to

LAUREN

Enjoy the x

(signature)

The Story of the NASCAR®-inspired Bobsled that Beat the World

Foreword

Steve Holcomb's Legacy

WHEN WE STARTED work on this book in early 2016, the athlete we thought would make the biggest contribution was Night Train pilot Steve Holcomb.

Why? Because Steve was the ultimate team player. After Steve's untimely death on May 6, 2017, we could look back and say we were right.

Bobsled fans and patriotic Americans remember Steve as the most successful USA bobsled athlete ever, as the man who in 2010 piloted the Night Train to the United States' first gold medal in the 4-man bobsled in 62 years and then, four years later, won two Olympic bronze medals in Sochi.

But our Bo-Dyn Project team remembers Steve as a technology geek who would fiddle with the computers and phones of both teammates and rivals until he fixed whatever

i

bug was gumming up the works. We remember Steve as the comedian who did the hilarious "Holcy" dance at bobsled tracks all over North America and Europe. We remember Steve as a man who could cross cultural boundaries and befriend fierce competitors like Germany's Andre Lange. And, yes, we remember Steve as a man who had an incredible sixth sense for getting a bobsled down a track.

But mostly, we remember Steve as the man who carried the Bo-Dyn Project over the finish line. There were times that, without the support of the U.S.' top driver, this project would have been cut short. It would have been far from a "failure" in the classic sense of the word—indeed, many of our sleds enjoyed success without Steve at the helm—but his belief in the Project and his talent for racing Bo-Dyn sleds are two big reasons why you are reading this book. Steve, along with his Night Train teammates Steve Mesler, Curt Tomasevicz, and Justin Olsen, rode the Night Train to perfection that February 2010 in Whistler; and we'll never forget that final run when the boys held on to win gold!

In the past year, Steve spoke with us several times in response to our requests to get this story down. He was always amenable to talk; always willing to go over those Olympic details that he had likely told the sports press and friends many times over. He even met us at a Lake Placid restaurant where both locals and tourists wanted to pose with his medals; which, of course, he was only too happy to do. Steve's insights into what made the sleds tick, the evolution of their development, and how he handled them on the mountain were enormously helpful to the final product you see here.

Steve was just 37 when he died at the Lake Placid Olympic Training Center, which served as his home, really, for almost two decades. Despite having won three Olympic medals and having been a six-time overall World Cup champion, Steve was far from finished competitively. He was all but assured to represent the U.S. at the Winter Games in PyeongChang, South Korea in February 2018. Steve never got there, and that is a tragedy, not just for U.S. bobsledding, but for all of his many friends and rivals who held him in such great esteem.

While Steve will go down as America's finest bobsled pilot ever, he will be long remembered for being, simply, a fine person.

Geoff Bodine and the Bo-Dyn Bobsled Project
Board of Directors

Prologue

What a Gold Medal Can Do

AN OLYMPIC GOLD medal can smooth over a lot of conflicts, mask a lot of pain. But can it fix things for good? When it comes to the Night Train, the bobsled that won 4-man Olympic gold for Team USA at the 2010 Vancouver Olympics, that depends on who you ask: the man who built it, the man who drove it, or the man who started it all — the man who dreamt it.

The Man Who Built It

Bob Cuneo has never ridden in a bobsled, much less pushed one at a sprint or driven one down a mountain at 80-90 miles per hour. Then again, Vince Lombardi never played a down in the NFL and Facebook founder, Mark Zuckerberg, is famously hard to be friends with.

In fact, upon meeting Cuneo, speed is the last thing that crosses one's mind. On a May 2016 afternoon in Oxford, Connecticut, inside "Cuneo's shop" as everyone from gold medal-winning bobsledders to NASCAR® champions refers to Chassis Dynamics, Cuneo was having some trouble even moving. The 69-year-old was due for a knee replacement in a few weeks, just another physical challenge in a life that has been filled with them. Cuneo traces his career as an engineer and designer to a childhood that changed forever when, as a three-old toddler, he simply collapsed, unable to walk. Part of his left femur had eroded and fallen apart. Years in a wheel chair and full body cast followed, until the fourth grade when a New York orthopedic surgeon used diced-up bone from Cuneo's tailbone to stitch together the two bones in his leg that were no longer connected.

Cuneo could walk, but while his friends played baseball and football, his leg wasn't strong enough for him to play sports. His playing fields, instead, became the family garage and driveway, where his mechanic father taught him everything there was to know about cars. By the time Cuneo was 12, he had worked on neighbors' cars for money. "Looking back, I think that experience affected me in two big ways," Cuneo says. "I had all the time in the world to learn

2

about cars, and I wanted to replace sports with another kind of competition. If I could build a race car that others could drive, I could be as competitive as anyone who played sports. In a way, I could be normal."

This day his pain is obvious as he struggles to navigate an office decorated with trophies, framed photos of winning race cars and bobsleds, and newspaper and magazine clippings. Cuneo points out the trophy given to him by Geoff Bodine (he's the man who dreamt it, and we'll get to him later) after Bodine had won the 1994 NASCAR Tyson 400 by a full lap — the last time a driver entered the winner's circle at least a full lap ahead of an entire field.

The irony of Cuneo's uneasy gait is that, for more than four decades, he has found speed where no other engineer or designer has even bothered to look. Whether it's a bobsled, a Sprint Cup Series race car, or the 1975 Toyota Celica GT he's currently restoring for a client, Cuneo's designs and innovations just make things go...well...*faster*. With the Night Train and its predecessor sleds dating all the way back to the early days of the Bo-Dyn Project in 1993 and 1994, Cuneo and his team of ragtag local fabricators and mechanics — dubbed "Team Provolone" by Cuneo in honor of one of his team's Italian heritage — achieved what big-time engineers from a

Who's Who of corporate giants like General Motors and General Electric could not: build American-made, superior equipment that no other country could match. "Look, there are lots of better engineers than me," Cuneo says. "But I know how to win!"

After easing himself down the staircase, Cuneo takes a visitor through the garage where he currently builds specialty cars for the rich and famous. He stops beside a frame for a Tucker sedan, not the '48 model that inspired the movie about the innovative auto designer Preston Tucker, but a Tucker car that was conceived but never built. Cuneo has been hired to bring the long-dormant design to life, alongside Preston Tucker's grandson, car designer Sean Tucker. That's the kind of project people hire Cuneo for. "A lot of people restore cars, but my niche is really high-performance cars," he says.

Next to the Tucker is the Celica GT, outfitted with a new, more powerful engine than the original four cylinders. "Somebody driving alongside this car at some point is going to be very surprised," Cuneo says of the Celica with just a hint of professional pride. "This will not be a normal '75 Celica." Cuneo is selective these days when it comes to his work. He's officially retired, which means he only works about 50 hours a week. "I'm an old guy, and I don't like deadlines," Cuneo says. He doesn't advertise, doesn't have a website, doesn't use social media, doesn't even try to get satisfied clients to evangelize for him. "As far as that stuff goes, I don't exist," Cuneo says. Why does he want it that way? Because when you're Bob Cuneo, people find you.

After all, this is the same garage where Cuneo outfit Paul Newman's race cars ("Paul loved to cook for all the guys," Cuneo says). The same garage which produced race cars that have won numerous NASCAR championships, four "24 Hours of Daytona" races, 15 national championships in the SCCA Series, and four national championships in the IMSA Series (helpful hint to aspiring racing fans: learn to love acronyms). This is the garage where Cuneo has built everything from military vehicles to drag racing cars.

So when his friend and race car royalty Bodine called him in 1992 with his crazy idea of using a NASCAR approach to building American-made bobsleds, Cuneo and his then partner, the late Bobby Vaillancourt, had to say yes to the challenge — they'd built just about every other kind of vehicle. So this garage is also where the Night Train was born, Bo-Dyn's crown jewel sled that dominated the sport of bobsledding from 2008 through 2010; when the team of pilot

Steve Holcomb and push athletes Steve Messler, Curt Tomasevicz, and Justin Olsen won just about everything there was to win, culminating in the first 4-man gold medal for the U.S. in 62 years.

"More than any one sled he did, I think Bob taught me how to think about technical problems," says Michael Nitsch, a German bobsled designer who was one of Cuneo's greatest professional rivals but also, tellingly, one of his best friends in the sport. Today Nitsch heads the bobsled division for Germany's FES sports agency, the German government-funded agency that researches and develops new equipment for German athletes of every Olympic sport. "The thing about Bob is he never had to be the smartest guy in the room. But a lot of time he was."

But for Cuneo and his team, the Bo-Dyn Project took a toll. The price paid for Night Train gold — as well as the other five Olympic medals won during the Bo-Dyn era — included the ridicule and skepticism emanating from some athletes about the initial Bo-Dyn Project designs, apathy from the United States Bobsled and Skelton Association (USBSF), an athlete-led cabal that tried to discredit Cuneo and his team, and even an attempt to filch Bo-Dyn technology by disassembling Bo-Dyn sleds in the company of representatives from other builders.

The greatest affront may have been after the Vancouver games when the USBSF made clear its stance that the Bo-Dyn Project really hadn't had much of an impact and that their involvement would be lessened going forward. It was a bitter pill to swallow after all the gratis work; after the long nights of trying to figure out a way for American sleds to go faster.

So the question is: Can the Night Train gold medal — not to mention the other Olympic and World Cup medals won during the Bo-Dyn era — validate it all? "You know, we did what Geoff Bodine set out to do," Cuneo reflects. "I think there is some ill-will about how it all ended, no doubt about it."

Later that night, Cuneo and his team gather at the Brookside Inn, the restaurant that stayed open for them after late nights working on the sleds; the restaurant where Cuneo and his team held scores of business meetings, the restaurant where anyone in the local area who knew anything about the Bo-Dyn Project came to celebrate the Night Train gold medal with a massive party during the Vancouver Olympics.

Cuneo and his friends sit outside. It gets cold, and everyone wants to go inside; but Cuneo is holding court, and the drinks are flowing. They tell stories of sleds being held hostage at checkpoints before European countries opened their borders, of going the wrong way down one-way European cobblestone streets, of smuggling a pair of bobsleds out of the Oslo Airport to get them to the Lillehammer Games in time.

So while a gold medal might not fix everything for Bob Cuneo, tonight he has the old team around him, talking about their greatest triumph. As he wanted to do 60 years ago, Cuneo competed. And he won on the world's biggest stage, showing that he was as good as anyone else. So that's one thing a gold medal can do.

*****

The Man Who Drove It

Steve Holcomb likes video games. In fact, he credits video games with making him a better bobsled pilot in 2016, at age 36, than he's ever been. The hand-eye coordination, the intense focus, the competition – all are elements of gaming that Holcomb believes helps his bobsled driving abilities. "I know, a great message for the kids," Holcomb says. "Play more video games if you want to be an Olympic athlete!"

As Holcomb likes to point out, however, he finds anything that replicates piloting a bobsled beneficial. Why? Because there just is not that much total time on a real track for bobsledders. Video games are a kind of simulator that augments practice time for Holcomb, whose mind manipulates numbers in the practiced way that one would expect from a man whose life's work is measured in hundredths of a second.

"Think about this way," Holcomb says. "During the season you get pretty much two minutes a day in runs. You get about 150 runs a year. That's 300 minutes a year or about five hours. As of 2016, I am the most experienced bobsled pilot on the World Cup circuit. And in my whole career, I've spent about 30 hours in total on a bobsled going down a real track."

In economic terms, then, there is a high barrier to entry to being a bobsled pilot, much more so than being a push athlete, which requires not deep knowledge of the sport but a lot of raw athleticism. The difficulty in becoming an experienced bobsled pilot is one reason why Holcomb – a year away from the South Korea Olympics – will likely be the pilot of USA-1 for an unprecedented third straight Olympics.

But even if he weren't still the top American pilot, even if upcoming drivers like Justin Olsen replaced him, Holcomb would still be the rock star of USA bobsledding, which actually isn't like being a rock star in the traditional sense at all. Holcomb doesn't make a habit of trashing hotel rooms and chooses to spend part of his off season in the decidedly uncool destination of East Tennessee State University, where he trains with his strength and conditioning coach. While bobsledders and other winter athletes from, say, Germany or Switzerland are recognizable stars, Holcomb can not only walk the streets of Manhattan unnoticed but the streets of Lake Placid, as well. But that can all change when he brings out the big guns – his Olympic medals.

On a March night in 2016, temperatures still frigid in the Adirondacks, Holcomb was at Nicola's, a favorite Italian family restaurant that he and the rest of the bobsled fraternity frequent when competition or training takes them to Lake Placid. The bartender at Nicola's is a friend, and Holcomb sits alone at the bar, not brandishing his medals out in the open yet. Besides the Vancouver gold, he's also packing his bronze medal from Sochi. Holcomb looks slightly uncomfortable as the bartender talks about how Olympic medals must serve as an aphrodisiac for the opposite sex. Holcomb offers, "That's not really true for me. But I am one of the world's great wing men."

Things at the bar are quiet until John Morgan walks in from a collegiate championship hockey game at the Olympic Arena across the street. Ask anyone from the bobsledding community who on the planet knows the most about the sport, and the same name always pops up – "John Morgan." Morgan is at once the sport's brashest promoter, its most well-versed historian, and the voice of the sport. He has been the Olympic bobsled color commentator for last nine Olympics Games for the USA networks, and for many years has had his own production and sports marketing company which packages and broadcasts World Cup bobsledding events. When a luger was tragically killed right before the Vancouver Olympics began, it was Morgan who NBC and many European broadcasters went to for perspective on the Vancouver track and how dangerous it was. Morgan even played himself in *Cool Runnings*, the film about the Jamaican bobsled team.

Morgan's connections to the sport go back to his father, Forrest "Dew Drop" Morgan, a former national bobsledding champion who managed the 1976 Olympic bobsled team. John Morgan himself, along with brothers Brian, Sean, and Jimmy, tried out for the 1980 Lake Placid Olympics as a 4-man team. They crashed and didn't make it. What some don't know about Morgan is the heavy price paid by his family for their love of the sport. Jimmy Morgan – who had been at the helm of USA-1 at the 1976 Winter Games in Innsbruck, Austria — was killed when his 4-man bobsled crashed at the World Bobsled Championships in Cortina, Italy in 1981. John, on assignment for ABC Sports in 1981, witnessed the crash.

Back at Nicola's, Morgan announces that Holcomb is in the house, urges him to take out his medals, and then the procession starts — the questions, the selfies, the trying on of the gold medal, in particular. Holcomb seems totally relaxed as the medal gets passed around the bar and a score of strangers examine it. Have any of Holcomb's medals ever disappeared during one of these late night show-and-tells? "No," he says. "It's sort of like some people with their kid. You can let it wander away a little bit, but you always have your eyes on it."

For years, it wouldn't have been so easy for Holcomb to have his eyes trained on his medals or anything else for that matter. In 2000, Holcomb was diagnosed with Keratoconus, a degenerative eye disease that affects 1 in 1,000 and leaves one in four blind if they do not choose to do a cornea transplant. Since he thought he could manage it, he didn't tell anyone.

In the months leading up to the 2002 Salt Lake City Winter Games — his home town Olympics — an injury forced Holcomb out of the Games. They say bad things come in threes, and the eye disease, the injury, and the fact of missing the Games brought on something entirely unfamiliar to Holcomb. As he put it in his memoir, *But Now I See:*

> *As days turned into weeks, and weeks to months, with no Olympic Games to get ready for, I felt the first pangs of something strange and heavy and dark. I would sit in the dark or stare at a computer screen as minutes slipped into hours. I didn't want to talk to anyone or see anyone. It hurt, but not like an injury, more like the ache you get with the flu.*

By spring 2007, it was clear to Holcomb and his doctors that he was slowly going blind. Even as he and his teammates experienced unprecedented success that winter season on the track by winning numerous World Cup races, things became darker, both literally and figuratively, for Holcomb. His eyesight became progressively worse, and he struggled with his secret, dreading a crash caused by his disease that could injure his teammates. According to his doctors, a cornea transplant was the only option offered to patients like Holcomb but, in Holcomb's mind, that was out of the question. The transplants would need to be done one eye at a time, with a recovery period of about two years for each procedure — a cure that would effectively end his career. It was in a hotel room in Colorado Springs after attending a sponsor event that Holcomb downed 73 sleeping pills and washed them down with a bottle of Jack Daniels Tennessee Whiskey. By all rights, this one-two combination should have killed just about anybody – couch potato or world-class athlete, large man or petite woman, 20-20 vision or 20-500 vision like Holcomb.

Holcomb didn't die, but he did experience a reincarnation. Amazed to be alive, he shortly after that told his coach, Brian Shimer, that he was legally blind. That December, a doctor named Brian Boxer Wachler performed an experimental procedure on Holcomb called C3-R, a noninvasive procedure that activates the vitamin riboflavin in the corneas through ultraviolet light. While to the uninitiated C3-R sounds like the ubiquitous "vitamin cures" that rain down on anxious, vulnerable cancer patients from well-meaning friends and family, this was a legitimate, but little-known, treatment that Dr. Boxer Wachler had been doing since 2004. The procedure stopped Holcomb's eyesight from getting worse until the following March when the same doctor surgically implanted a lens behind the lens of each eye. For those who wear contacts, think of it as wearing permanent contacts. The revolutionary treatment is now known as the Holcomb C3-R.

From 2008 on, Holcomb and his Night Train teammates were unstoppable, winning the World Championships in Lake Placid in 2009 before claiming gold in Vancouver in 2010 — the first men's bobsled gold for the American men in 62 years. "You know we have about 68 races in four years, and the Olympics is just one race out of all of them," Holcomb says. "One race in four years. I dreamed of gold as a kid. When I first ski raced, that's what I dreamed would happen."

And then it happened, and Holcomb didn't know what to feel after everything he'd been through. In a way, he still doesn't. "After we crossed the line, and we won, and everyone was cheering, it didn't really sink in," Holcomb says. "Coming in, you don't want to put too much pressure on yourself. I was thinking before the last heat that I've done this a thousand times; just do it again. If you treat this one race like it's this huge thing, if you say to yourself, 'Oh my God I'm at the Olympics,' that's when you screw up. But it's a double-edged sword, too, trying to treat it like any other race. I mean, to this day, I don't really think it's sunk in that I'm an Olympic gold medalist."

So if it hasn't really sunk in yet, what can a gold medal do for Steve Holcomb? It doesn't keep away the "dark periods" as Holcomb calls them; that's up to him. And it didn't stop his blindness; Dr. Boxer Wachler did that. But could Olympic gold help others see? With his gold medal, Holcomb today has the pulpit to spread the word about the Holcomb C3-R treatment that, along with Tommy John surgery, is one of the few medical procedures named after an athlete.

"It's sort of crazy," Holcomb offers at Nicola's as the restaurant patrons continue to ask about his medal. "If any of these people had keratoconus, their doctors wouldn't tell them about this treatment. There are lots of reasons why people don't want to disrupt the status quo. But this is now a

16

proven treatment, and I think it's up to me to get the word out." Steve Holcomb: medical pioneer, disruptor of the status quo. So that's something else a gold medal can do.

*****

The Man Who Dreamt It

Bobsledders are big men. Step into the athletes' waiting area at the top of the hill at a World Cup bobsled race, and one might just mistake it for the locker room of a Division I college football team.

The sport's rules provide limits on the total weight for a bobsled and four men together, and since momentum — needed to overcome drag and friction — equals mass times velocity, a 4-man bobsled team wants to get as close to that weight limit as possible. Before weight limits were placed on sleds in the early 1950s, in fact, bobsledders were downright huge, seeing as the rules of gravity were the same back then.

Geoff Bodine, on the other hand, is not a physically big man. The first time he ever tried bobsledding himself, in fact, "I nearly fell out of the back of the sled. I'm a little guy, and I was being thrown all over the place." The 1986 Daytona winner, now 67, is small and wiry, a ball of kinetic energy as he describes over dinner the reason why he founded the Bo-

Dyn Project back in 1992. Even though he's a household name due to his racing exploits, Bodine, as much as anyone, seems to realize that his ultimate legacy may be as much the Bo-Dyn Bobsled Project as anything he did behind the wheel of a race car. The reason for that is simple: driving was for himself, his family; his team. Bo-Dyn? That was for the country.

Bodine has told the story a hundred times to a hundred journalists: how he was watching the 1992 Winter Games in Albertville on television during a break of a race week, listening to Morgan's trademark enthusiastic commentary. Today, nearly 25 years after the fact, Bodine still expresses real outrage at what he heard. Morgan was describing the sorry state of the bobsled program at the time, which included athletes having to purchase their own equipment, most often used sleds from their European counterparts. "I found from listening to John Morgan that our athletes weren't using American-made equipment, and I'm a proud American," Bodine says. "Then I found out the athletes had to pay for their own equipment, and I couldn't believe that. I mean, I'd never heard anything like that. Can you imagine another sport at a world-class level where they made them buy their own equipment? Fortunately, I was in a position to do something about it. I had made some money through racing, and I wanted to help by building American-made sleds we could be proud of. There was never any idea about profit; it was about providing equipment that was good enough to win with."

And the truth, which Bodine didn't know at the time of that fateful Olympic telecast from Albertville, was even worse than he thought. Tuffy Latour, today the coach on the U.S. skeleton team and a bobsled pilot back in the late 1980s and 1990s, describes a scene where athletes would go to pick from sorry, discarded equipment, akin to a weekend hacker picking out a set of rental golf clubs. "When I first came in the sport, you walked into the sled shed in Lake Placid, and there were sleds everywhere just really beat up, you know, just a bucket of bolts," Latour says. "You went through and picked your sled. Before Bodine came around, people were always scrambling to put sleds together, and I think it was part of the culture back then. It was every man for himself."

Why did Bodine go to Cuneo? Bodine came to know Cuneo from racing against the cars that his future partner built. Bodine grew up in upstate Chemung, New York, near Elmira in the western part of the state, but raced everywhere in the Northeast. Connecticut, associated in the minds of many Americans with New York City bedroom communities, finance types, and country clubs, actually has a long and storied racing history. Well-known race car tracks dot the state, and these were the tracks that Bodine crisscrossed as a young racer: Bridgeport, Lebanon Valley, Plainville, Candlelight Park. "What happened was we all grew up in this car culture," says Frank Briglia, one of Cuneo's key team members through the years. "The racing community up here really gets to know one another, and that's how we came to know Geoff – Bob, myself, and Bobby Vaillancourt. Geoff was one of the biggest drivers doing the races around here."

It didn't take Bodine long to recognize that the Chassis Dynamics team, rough around the edges as some of its team members were, had major engineering chops. "I've designed race cars, I drove them, I maintained them," Bodine says. "And when I decided that our athletes should have American-made sleds, that's where I went." The Bo-Dyn Project takes its name from the combination of Bodine's name ("Bo") and Chassis Dynamics ("Dyn"). A true partnership it was, even down to the fact that at various times from 1992 through the next decade and a half, the Bo-Dyn Project sucked time and money from both of them. "I've said it a number of times,"

Cuneo says. "Geoff ruined my life with that first phone call to me about wanting to build American-made sleds."

But Bodine was the one funding out of his pocket at the beginning. The first budget back in the early 1990s was $25,000. In under a month, the call came from Cuneo and Vaillancourt. They needed more money in the budget, so Bodine put in another $25,000. By the time the first bobsled had been built and tested in Calgary in time for the 1994 Lillehammer Games, Bodine had put in approximately $150,000 of his money.

At the same time, the bureaucracy at the USBSF grew nervous that a big-time race driver and his engineering partners had entered, with some fanfare, their cloistered world, even though the newcomers were providing the funds and the engineering talent to deliver the American athletes new sleds. "I was blind-sided," Bodine says. "I thought, man; they will welcome us with open arms and try to guide us. But it was just the opposite." In some ways, one can't blame the USBSF Board, which had only been recently reconstituted. For decades, various supposed saviors of American bobsledding had come along, only to lose interest or fail spectacularly. So when a famous race car driver came along, it's not that surprising that the sport's governing body thought Bodine's interest in bobsledding wouldn't last much longer than a Daytona 500 pit stop.

Eventually, Bodine had to turn off the financial spigot. The same generosity of resources that Bodine showed to the Bo-Dyn Project didn't produce as good results in another arena. He stopped winning races, eventually undergoing serious financial hardship. The Bo-Dyn Project survived thanks to key partners like Whelen Engineering, a Bodine race car sponsor that became the main sponsor of the Bo-Dyn Project for years, a relationship forged by a now-vice president at Whelen, Phil Kurze.

Meanwhile, life threw Bodine the kind of curve balls most people see maybe once in a lifetime. Bodine went through a divorce, his ex-wife's death, and the death of a girlfriend. Bodine nearly died himself; in February 2000, he suffered through one of the most horrific-looking crashes racing fans have ever witnessed at the same Daytona International Speedway in a truck racing event. The way Bodine tells it, his late father told him it wasn't time and turned him back from heaven's gates.

After everything, Bodine today, like Cuneo and Holcomb, is alive and well. He's ready for his next challenge. It likely won't be as epic as the Bo-Dyn Project, and it certainly won't result in Olympic gold. But that's okay because, for Bodine, his mission is complete. The funny part? For Bodine, it was never about the gold medal. "I was never one to say, 'We have to win gold, or this was not successful,' Bodine says. "To me it was, did we do right by these kids? Did we give them a chance to win? And I think we did that."

Chapter One

Geoff Bodine Gets an Idea

FOR RACING LEGEND Geoff Bodine, it was a nice day off from his jammed schedule of NASCAR races. He was comfortably settled into his living room at home near Greensboro, North Carolina, watching the 1992 Olympic Winter Games from Albertville, France.

Bodine had loved the Olympics since he was a child growing up in upstate Chemung, New York, near the Pennsylvania border. Looking back to that ABC Olympic telecast, Bodine recalls that it was the first bobsled competition he had ever watched closely.

Who was Bodine watching? Team USA had some amazing athletes. There was Brian Shimer, one of the most talented bobsled pilots in U.S. history; as of spring 2017, the head coach of the U.S. men's bobsled team. Herschel Walker, the famed football star who was part of an early 1990s phenomenon of track stars and football stars like Willie Gault, Edwin Moses, and Walker trying their hands at bobsledding, was Shimer's brakeman in the 2-man competition. Walker blew everyone way in the bobsled training "combine," where athletes are tested on a variety of speed and power tests, as well as in the Olympic push trials.

Walker was legendary for his workouts, which consisted of punishing sessions of thousands of pushups and sit-ups. Shimer roomed with Walker and remembers wondering deep into the night if the grunting noises rising from the hotel room floor would ever cease. "That's all he ever did, pushups and sit-ups," Shimer says. "I don't remember him ever really sleeping. I can attest he exercised at all hours of the day and night."

But, unfortunately for Team USA, all of that effort didn't end up transferring to the actual races at the Albertville Games. Walker's sprinting speed didn't translate well to the ice, and then there was that little matter of actually getting *into* the sled. Once Walker qualified for the Olympics based on his push times, Shimer and the coaches had about three weeks to teach the former Heisman Trophy winner how to push a sled on the ice and how to hop in cleanly. To top it all off, the duo's first heat in the Olympics was their very first race together in competition. "Herschel was certainly the best athlete of all the bobsledders there, but he wasn't the best bobsledder in the world because he hadn't learned to be a bobsledder yet," Shimer says today. According to Morgan, "Walker was the most athletic physical specimen the sport had ever seen, but he needed another 3-4 weeks, and a couple of races, to really be world-class in the sport."

With Bodine watching at home, both U.S.A. 2- and 4-man teams were struggling. In the 2-man event, one team finished way back in 24th place. The other team – USA-1 – featuring Shimer and brakeman Walker — finished 7th. As they crossed the finish line, CBS bobsled color commentator John Morgan said something that immediately struck Bodine: "The U.S. has not medaled in bobsled since 1956, and they probably will not until they start building their own sleds," Morgan said. In the 4-man competition, the USA sleds finished in 9th and 11th places respectively. For a racing connoisseur such as Bodine, it was painful to witness their imprecise maneuverings.

With no successful American sled-maker, U.S. athletes purchased used equipment from their European competitors once their foes were ready to move on to new sleds. Even more unbelievable, there was no central budget from the United States Olympic Committee (USOC) or the United States Bobsled and Skeleton Federation (USBSF) to purchase these bobsleds (the USBSF is the governing body for both bobsled and skeleton, skeleton being a sliding sport in which the participant lies prone on a small sled while going down the track). Athletes had to scrimp somehow and save to buy their own bobsleds, which appalled Bodine.

Simply put, the U.S. team went into the Olympics using bobsleds that already put them in a huge hole before the first sled had even gone down the hill. Bodine's immediate outrage sparked the simple idea: American-made sleds provided to U.S. bobsledders at no cost so that they could compete with the best in the world.

"I had no grand plan about gold medals for these athletes or anything like that," Bodine says today. "It was just this idea that wouldn't it be great if these athletes got some decent American-made equipment so they could just concentrate on their sport."

Bodine's powerful idea would not only change American bobsledding forever but also usher in worldwide a new breed of sleds, greatly influenced by the NASCAR culture that Bodine would bring to this endeavor. But first, it's worth asking this question: how did U.S. bobsledding come to this moment in 1992 when a man completely new to the sport had to save it for his country?

A Brief History: Winter Playgrounds and Bureaucratic Playpens

Considering the sleek lines and buff exteriors of today's bobsleds, the sport's roots are charmingly simple: the first bobsleds were fashioned in the 1880s when Swiss tobogganers attached two together and applied a simple steering mechanism. It took another decade for the first bobsled club to be formed, in 1897 in the winter playground of St. Moritz. While Switzerland may be the home of bobsledding, the United States adopted the sport early on.

The history of bobsledding is very much connected with the history of northern New York, as the 1932 Lake Placid Games sparked the construction of the only bobsled track in North America at the time, a status it would have for more than 50 years. The original Lake Placid track, today the only bobsled track on the National Register of Historic Places, is generally known as one of the most challenging in the world. Shimer remembers going down it as a driver for the first time, following the 1988 Calgary Games. Calgary has a very forgiving track and is a favorite venue for new drivers to train. With Shimer accustomed to the relatively gentle turns of Calgary, his maiden trip down the Lake Placid track with its high, hairpin turns ended with a crash into a wall that totaled his sled and ripped the right side of his helmet off. "This was my Olympic helmet, and there wasn't a scratch on it," Shimer says. "It was going on my mantle. We hit the wall so hard it just blew right apart."

Shimer wasn't the first big name in Olympic bobsledding, of course. The earliest bobsled champion in the U.S. was Billy Fiske, whose name now adorns the trophy given to the 4-man U.S. champions each year. Fiske was the scion of a prominent New York banking family who took up bobsledding when he was sent to boarding school in Europe. Fiske won gold in what was then the 5-man competition in St. Moritz in 1928 at just 16 years of age, which to this day makes him the youngest gold medalist in the history of the sport.

After the St. Moritz Olympics, Fiske lent this celebrity to popularizing the new ski resort town of Aspen, Colorado, further cementing his winter sports renown. When it came time for the 1932 Olympics in Lake Placid, Fiske was chosen to carry the U.S. flag into the opening ceremonies. A few days later, he repeated his St. Moritz gold medal win, piloting the 4-man team to victory. Morgan, who has an encyclopedic knowledge of the sport, cherishes one special story related to Fiske: when Morgan's father was a small boy, his grandfather took him to the 1932 Lake Placid Olympic Games 4-man bobsled awards ceremony, where Fiske gave the boy an affectionate rub on the head for good luck. "When you talk American bobsledding royalty, that's Billy Fiske," Morgan says today.

From his school days in Europe, Fiske's affection for the British was so great that when World War II engulfed England in 1940, he abandoned a promising banking career (he wrote to his sister that the British had always been good to him, and he couldn't just sit in New York "making dough"). Pretending to be Canadian, Fiske became one of just 11 Americans to join the Royal Air Force Volunteer Reserve, becoming part of the legendary "Millionaires' Squadron." Fiske ended up being one of the first Americans to be killed in action in World War II when a Luftwaffe pilot shot up his plane during the Battle of Britain, the week's-long dogfight over London that stopped Hitler's plan to add England to his collection of European conquests. Fiske's final act of heroism was landing his plane intact even as the life drained out of his body, 80% of which had been badly burned from an exploded gas tank, one of the only flaws of the legendary British Spitfire planes. The Luftwaffe was destroying so many British planes that each and every aircraft was desperately needed. The British buried Fiske with honor in Boxgrove Priory, England with the epitaph: "An American citizen who died that England might live." A plaque also exists at the legendary St. Paul's Cathedral in London with the same words.

While Fiske occupies a singular niche in U.S. bobsledding – he was a true citizen of the world and a genuine American hero both on and off the track— other Americans made huge contributions to the sport as well. In fact, decades before Geoff Bodine would try to resurrect American sled design, the U.S. had a reputation for bobsled innovation. Bob Linney, a Yale graduate from the Adirondack mining town of Lyon Mountain, designed a sled he called "Iron Shoes[1]" because of its cast-iron runners. It was the first all-metal bobsled, built completely from materials mined at Lyon Mountain. Like the Bo-Dyn Project, Linney's motivation was patriotism, as he convinced the owners of Chateaugay Ore and Iron Co., where he worked as an engineering foreman, to fund the project so the U.S. could win the 4-man gold at the Winter Olympics in Germany and show up Hitler in his back yard.

---

[1] Adirondack Life, "February 1980, "Iron Shoes."

"Iron Shoes," at 11 feet, 7 inches long, with Linney driving, won the North American bobsled championship at Lake Placid in January 1936, an astounding eight seconds ahead of the nearest competitor. The sled was shipped to Germany for the Games, but, alas, arrived too late for 4-man pilot Hubert Stevens to practice with it, and Stevens and his team eventually wound up finishing 4th on a different sled. World War II stopped Iron Shoes and her sister sleds from competing in the Olympic Games in 1940, of course, but its innovations changed the sports forever.

In 1936, however, another upstate New York team did strike gold in Germany. Ivan Brown of Keene Valley, a lesser-known Adirondack burgh than Lake Placid but one with its nearby high peaks, took home gold with Alan Washbond. It would be the last U.S. gold medal in the men's 2-man, to this day.

After World War II, a U.S. team won the 4-man in the 1948 Games, that were held back in St. Moritz. After that, however, the European alpine nations started dominating bobsledding with their mountain culture and access to numerous excellent tracks. The Americans thought things would change when the 1960 Games was awarded to Squaw Valley, California. Here was a chance to parlay the Games into a new bobsled track and breathe new life into the sport in the U.S. But just nine nations committed to the competition by 1958, and the organizing committee couldn't get the internal support to build the track. Bobsled was out for the 1960 Olympics, which threw the sport into a tailspin in the U.S. for the next 20 years with no new track, little funding, and little exposure for the sport. Failing to get the support needed to build an Olympic bobsled track in Squaw Valley was one of many failures not of American bobsled athletes, but American amateur sports organizers and officials. Another example was when the U.S. Bobsled Federation mishandled an effort by General Motors in the mid-1960s to build American-made sleds. The bobsled powers-that-be rushed portions of the project, leading to a crash in St. Moritz that GM felt gave the project a black eye. As Morgan puts it, the company picked up their ball and went home: "General Motors packed up their sleds after that, and no one in the sport ever saw them again."

The medal drought and bureaucratic chaos continued throughout the 1960's, 1970's and 80s, even with the completion of the Calgary track for the 1988 Olympics, which gave Americans another North American track at which to train. In 1991, things came to a head when the USBSF made news twice for the wrong reasons. First, in the spring of 1991, the USOC found serious accounting improprieties in the USBSF finances, including some Swiss Bank accounts. Also in the spring of 1991, after an article headlined "*Ice Follies*" appeared in *Sports Illustrated*, the USOC disbanded the USBSF Board of Directors. Later that year, another incident surfaced about the selection to the 1992 US Olympic team, and a grievance was filed by NFL players Willie Gault, Greg Harrell and track superstar Edwin Moses against the USBSF for allegedly not creating a level playing field for the athletes trying out for the Albertville Games. It was into this pool of disarray and failure that Geoff Bodine was contemplating diving headfirst.

A Life-Changing 24 Hours in Lake Placid

Bodine is starting to tell friends and colleagues that he has this idea about building American bobsleds. As he likes to tell it, he told one friend too many, an optometrist named Bill Stroud, whom he had known since they were teens in upstate New York. The two attended nearby high schools, raced cars together, and raised hell together. When Bodine was racing cars around mall parking lots with the Sports Car Club of Watkins Glen, Stroud was there too. The pair ended up living not far from each other in North Carolina and on a day not long after the Albertville Olympics, Stroud listened to Bodine say how stacked the deck was against the American bobsledders and how bad their equipment was compared to that of other nations. So Stroud, who had visited Lake Placid a few times over the years, challenged Bodine to do something.

"Well, why don't we go to Lake Placid and check it out?" Stroud suggested to Bodine. Bodine, in the middle of a full-time racing season, ran through the litany of his upcoming races, from Daytona to Rockingham. He couldn't make the commitment. "There's no way I have time," Bodine told Stroud, thinking that was the end of it.

But, as it turned out, Stroud was intrigued as well. He, too, had watched the Americans' dismal performance in Albertville on television and thought his friend, an expert on racing if there ever was one, was on to something. Stroud reached out to a friend who had his own airplane. Stroud went back to Bodine and suggested they fly to Lake Placid on a Monday, and come back the following day. A piece of cake.

Bodine was still worried about his racing schedule, so Stroud just went ahead and set up the trip. Stroud called officials in Lake Placid and announced that Geoff Bodine, 1986 Daytona champ, was interested in learning more about

American bobsledding and wanted to travel up to Lake Placid to go for a ride in a bobsled. Their answer came quickly: "When can he come?"

"Bill told me, 'Look I've taken care of everything. Just show up at the airport,'" Bodine says. "If Bill Stroud hadn't just gone ahead and set it all up, there would never have been a single Bo-Dyn bobsled," Bodine says. "Never. There was no way I was going up to Lake Placid. It was racing season!"

As long as he was going to hurtle down a mountain in a bobsled, Bodine – who understood the sports media as well as anyone after a long career spent both in the winner's circle – asked his public relations adviser to notify ESPN and whatever other high-profile media would go up to Lake Placid. On the appointed day, he and his then-wife, Kathy Bodine, showed up at the airport — but there was a snafu. A winter storm was coming into the Adirondack Mountains where the village of Lake Placid is nestled in the high peaks. It wasn't certain the plane would get up to the area in time to beat the worst of the storm. If that was the case, the plan was to simply turn around and go back, and someone else could worry about the future of American bobsledding. Bodine's party eventually landed in the middle of the blizzard, snow piled up on the runway. "If we had been another 15 minutes later, there would have been no way we would have been able to land," Stroud says.

One of Bodine's first stops was the Olympic Training Center that houses all manner of U.S. winter sports athletes. One of them was skeleton athlete Dave Kurtz, who would become the biggest early champion of the Bo-Dyn Project and today is the head of para bobsledding in the U.S. Earlier that day, Kurtz had been in a bad accident as he crossed the finish line at the U.S. National Skeleton Championship, Kurtz' last event as a competitor, as he planned to retire. "Geoff came up to say hi, and the bruises on my face were all fresh and raw," Kurtz says. "I think he looked and me and probably wondered what he was getting into."

When they arrived at the track at Mount Van Hoevenberg, it was clear that word had gotten out about the little bobsledding exhibition. CBS Sports and ESPN were both present to capture for posterity Bodine riding in the back of a 2-man sled driven by U.S.A. bobsled pilot Bruce Rosselli.

In 1992, the second modern track used today was still almost a decade away from being christened. As mentioned earlier, Lake Placid's original track is to its modern cousin what an old, rickety wooden roller coaster is to today's newfangled coasters with tubular steel tracks and polyurethane wheels. The old track's design, from many decades ago, features sharp turns and long straightaways that generate tremendous speed. Morgan, born and raised in the Lake Placid area, grew up watching his uncle and father on the track, says the old Lake Placid track was among the most challenging in the world and had great respect from the Europeans, much as Darlington generates enormous respect from NASCAR drivers. "If you don't know what you're doing, there's no doubt about it, you're going to crash in those hairpin turns," Morgan says.

Modern sleds and athletes were too fast for the old track; and it was so dangerous, in fact, that by 1992, the USBSF didn't even hold official international competitions there anymore. But no one told Bodine that. "No, nobody explained that to me how dangerous it was," Bodine recalls with a laugh. "I guess they thought I was this big famous race car driver, so what would I be afraid of?"

When bobsled athletes are first learning the sport, they don't start runs from the very top of the hill; instead, they begin two-thirds or even half-way down the track. But with Rosselli driving, the idea was to give Bodine the full treatment. Bodine walked up the track with Rosselli –

"walking the track" is a standard practice for a team before a run – the whole time wondering whether it wouldn't make more sense to walk *down* the track, since that's the way the bobsled goes.

At the top, Bodine noticed various bobsled athletes jogging in place and otherwise warming up for their own practice runs. Bodine approached one athlete and asked, as the brakeman, what exactly was he supposed to do? "Oh, you know, the snow and ice are all broken up down there at the bottom," the man replied with a smile. "Just pull back on those handles a little; you won't have a problem." Bodine noticed that, in fact, a bunch of people at the top had big smiles on their faces. "I just thought they were very friendly," he recalls. One even called out to Bodine, in what Bodine thought was the equivalent of an actor telling another to break a leg, "Hey, your chin is going to meet your knees today." It turns out he meant it.

What people don't realize about bobsledding is the physical toll a run takes on both a sled and its human occupants – never mind the potential dangers of crashing. Even the smoothest runs give a sled a pounding, and taking those bumps and turns at 60 or 70 miles an hour inevitably leaves athletes battered with various bruises. Concussions related to contact sports are a major issue today. But head injuries can also happen in bobsledding, with the constant jostling of the head as the sled makes its twists and turns down the track.

As the television producers were setting up for the recording of the ride – "GoPros" were a couple of decades away from being invented, so the brakeman had to press "record" on the recorder on his lap in order for the camera mounted on the pilot's helmet to start recording – Bodine was wondering what he was getting himself into. For one thing, as a small man, he was having trouble reaching the break handles.

"I could tell Geoff was nervous," Stroud says. So, enjoying the kind of relationship that lifelong friends tend to have, Stroud walked up to the 2-man sled in which Bodine was occupying the back seat. Stroud leaned over to Bodine. "Don't worry, Kathy (Bodine's then-wife) is at the finish line, and she has a fresh set of underwear for you."

Bodine was still figuring out how to use the brake handles when they received the push-off and were heading down the mountain (a real 2-man or 4-man bobsled race starts, of course, with the team pushing its own sled). They started picking up speed. And then more speed. And Bodine suddenly realized he was starting to slide toward the back of the sled. "On those old racing sleds there wasn't much of a ledge on the back to hold you in," he recounts. "I'm thinking, 'Holy Cow; I'm going to fall off of this thing.'"

When Rosselli hit the corner nicknamed "Zig Zag," the downward force doubled Bodine over, indeed sending his chin onto his knees, as the jokesters at the top of the track had foretold. In another prank, some of the other hangers-on had also told Bodine to make sure to stick his head up and keep watch where the sled was going — precisely the opposite of what he was supposed to do. "I'm looking all over the place, and my head is getting jerked from side-to-side, smashing the sides of the sled," Bodine says. "That's when I realized they'd again been messing with me, so I put my head down!"

As the pair went around the final corner, Bodine could hear Rosselli yell "brake!" Bodine grabbed the brake handles and pulled them, but they slipped right out of his hands. Since the stop area was tiered, Bodine kept losing his grip on the brake handles as the sled repeatedly hit the equivalent of multiple speed bumps. And they still weren't slowing down! A TV crew member working in the "stop" area assumed that a sled driven by Rosselli would indeed stop when it was supposed to and didn't move as the sled bore down on him. A track worker had to alertly grab the TV staffer and jump out of the way. With Rosselli repeatedly screaming, "Brake," Bodine finally gained a purchase on the brake handles and pulled with all his might. The sled passed through the entire "stop" area, narrowly missing a huge boulder that, for some reason, was in the vicinity. They came to a stop in a snow bank. Rosselli leaped out laughing; Bodine got out and announced, "Hey that was incredible! But once is enough."

But Rosselli had other ideas. In front of the small crowd that gathered while the pair were doing their television interviews, Rosselli suggested they go again. Bodine looked down at his wrist, checking an imaginary wristwatch. "Oh, I don't think we have time; we have to get going," Bodine responded. The chorus all around him announced: "You've got plenty of time; go ahead!" While it might seem glamorous, there are times in life when being a famous race car driver has its disadvantages. This was one of those times. "Hell, I couldn't say no," Bodine says today. "I'm a macho race car driver!"

Back at the top of the mountain, Bodine was now truly terrified because he knew what was coming. Being in an open-air sled going 70 miles an hour through tight corners was, as it turned out, much different than driving a race car 200 miles per hour. For one thing, a race car driver enjoys the protection of being strapped in a harness. This time, Bodine told himself, he would pull those brake handles no matter what. And he did it so well that the next invitation from Rosselli was to drive the sled.

"Are you crazy? I'll kill us!" Bodine told Rosselli. But Rosselli walked him to the half-mile chute where new drivers start and explained where to go and what to do. This time Bodine wouldn't be in charge of the brake handles, but instead the steering rings, which are attached to a rope-and-pulley system that connects to the front runners. A subtle tug on a ring moves the sled in that direction. They were pushed off. Bodine cleared the first few turns and then negotiated the dreaded Zig Zag. He went down the straight away and then around the last corner. He had done it! Now it was Bodine's turn to suggest another run. "I had this big head now," Bodine said. "I thought I was a bobsled driver!"

The push came on the next run, and Bodine waved at the crowd as he went through an early turn. But almost immediately Bodine realized he had, by dumb luck, picked the right "line" the previous trip down, a "line" being what a pilot calls his path through the turns and down the track. This time, Bodine's line was way off. He realized he had no idea what he was doing. "I just went blank," he recalls. "It was a form of panic!"

Bodine came late off the corner from Zig Zag and nearly rolled the sled over. There's a lot of noise as one flies down the mountain in a bobsled, and Bodine couldn't hear Rosselli reminding him to turn off the corners earlier. In the straightway before the last corner, Bodine prayed that he wouldn't kill Rosselli or someone watching if the sled left the track. Not wanting to come off the corner late, Bodine guided the steering ring way too early. The last corner at Lake Placid's old track is so wide that even experienced pilots through the years would get impatient and turn off early. Bodine's early action drove the front of the sled into the wall, and the subsequent rebound then slammed the back end into the wall, knocking the wind out of Rosselli. On the video, Rosselli can be heard saying, "Oh shit!"

As the sled mercifully came to a stop and the final interviews with the media commenced, Rosselli called Bodine over to the sled. He pointed to the back of the bobsled. The back end hit the wall so hard it had bent the frame six inches to the left. "The sled was destroyed," Bodine says. With his adrenaline off the run still fresh, having experienced the sport as few non-Olympians ever had, and having crashed a U.S. Olympic bobsled, Bodine turned to Rosselli. "Well, Bruce," Bodine sighed, "I guess I'll have to build you a bobsled."

In his time, Bodine had done just about everything in racing, including designing his own race car. But that kind of knowledge came after years in the sport. Bodine was not by profession an engineer or professional designer. He knew this was a job for the ultimate pro.

Chapter Two

Imagining a NASCAR Sled

GEOFF BODINE KNEW – or at least was pretty sure – that he could get a bobsled built. He would work on the 2-man sled first and then eventually the marquee 4-man sled. After all, he'd been building his own race cars for years, and Bodine figured they were a heck of a lot more complicated than a damn sled.

But Bodine will admit today that he may not have been exactly thinking straight that day in Lake Placid when he told Bruce Roselli that he would build him a new sled. Fear will do that to a man, even to one of the history's most decorated race car drivers. "I'll be honest, if I hadn't bent Bruce's frame, I might have never gotten involved," Bodine says. "Remember, I almost had wrecked twice already. There was fear and the shock of what just happened. I wasn't thinking straight, but that's what came out."

A vague idea that Americans should have world-class, American-built sleds had turned into a promise. Even though Bodine realized almost immediately that he might be in over his head, his world view wouldn't allow him to turn back. "I'm a man of integrity," Bodine says. "When you say something – when your lips are moving, and something comes out – you're supposed to do it."

Bodine also wanted to keep his word because he already felt a growing kinship to bobsledders. The most important skills in racing cars are choosing the right lines and reacting quickly. During his short stay in Lake Placid, Bodine had developed enormous respect for bobsled athletes regarding these two talents. With no numbers on the wall, no markings on the track, and nothing to indicate when to turn, bobsledders fly down a chute of ice with only the pilot's nerve and instincts to get them to the bottom. Bobsledding, in a sense, was more old-school, more *pure* even, than car racing. The skill isn't just to go fast; the real trick for the pilot is to move the sled down the track so that when it comes off the corners, everyone doesn't wind up in the hospital. "In bobsledding, you learn the track, and you pick the line,"

Bodine says in describing why he so admires the physical courage of bobsledders. "As a race car driver, I had a ton of respect for what these men and women did after trying it first-hand in Lake Placid."

But the sport's diehards present in Lake Placid that day had seen dilettantes come and go. Says John Morgan, "I guarantee you that most of the people on the mountain figured Geoff would go back to sunny North Carolina and never be heard from again."

When Bodine got back home and told his family what he'd promised, they were all for it. But he was racing every week; his support team and mechanics were busy. How could he possibly pull this off? He turned to Bob Cuneo and Bobby Vaillancourt – two friends and veteran race car designers with whom Bodine had a long history.

Cuneo and Viallancourt had gotten to know Bodine back in the late 1970s, mostly from eating Bodine's dust. In 1978, Cuneo was building race cars out of his shop, and one of his drivers was Vaillancourt. Each weekend on a different New England or Upstate New York track, Bodine – who, unlike Vaillancourt, already had a major sponsor — would finish first with Vaillancourt close behind. Between races, Cuneo would improvise, much as he would decades later with the Bo-Dyn sleds. But Bodine was in the middle of a historic season as a modified driver, gaining entrance into the Guinness Book of World Records for "most wins in a season," with 55 wins out of 84 events started. "Geoff and Bobby separated themselves from the field, but every week he'd just be a little better," Cuneo says.

After the season, when Bodine decided to move down south and move up a class in competition, Cuneo and Vaillancourt paid him a visit out of respect for their superior foe. "Everybody had been so focused at the track on winning; we never spent that much time being friendly," Cuneo says. "But we had such great respect for him that we wanted to wish him well."

At what was supposed to be a send-off, Bodine mentioned how happy Cuneo and Vaillancourt must be that Bodine wouldn't be around. But Cuneo responded that, on the contrary, they wished he was sticking around so they could "kick his butt." After a few laughs, the trio came up with the idea to join forces and build a car no one could beat.

So with the combination of Bodine's driving skills and Chassis Dynamics design prowess, the Bo-Dyn name was forged, years before it would be associated with bobsledding. The White Tornado, as it was called, would become a feared sight on the NASCAR modified circuit as Bodine drove it to a winning percentage of more than 70% in 1979. Moreover, this was against some of the toughest competition that division had ever seen. "That car just beat everyone, and it became one of Geoff's favorite cars ever," Cuneo says.

With that shared history, Bodine knew exactly what Cuneo and Vaillancourt could bring to his bobsled project. Sure, building race car chassis – not bobsleds — was their business, but that was exactly why Bodine wanted them. He had raced with them, and against them, and built race cars with them. What was more, Bodine knew there was a lull in the race car business, particularly for Chassis Dynamics, the Connecticut home of which was 1,000 miles north of where most of the top-notch action was.

All in all, Bodine's call came to Cuneo and Vaillancourt at exactly the right time. Cuneo characterizes the fateful phone call from Bodine this way: "It is a true story that sounds not true." When Bodine called, it was Vaillancourt who answered. It had been months since Bodine had talked to the team at Chassis Dynamics. "Hey, it's Geoff," Bodine told Vaillancourt. "I bet you don't know why I'm calling." "Yeah, I do," Vaillancourt shot back. "But I haven't said anything yet," Bodine responded. "You can't know why I'm calling." "We saw it on ESPN," came the reply. "You went for a ride on a bobsled. You want us to build you a bobsled, don't you?"

Not only had Cuneo and Vaillancourt watched Geoff on television during his great Lake Placid adventure, but they had also seen him say on national TV how appalled he was that American sliders were using inferior cast-off sleds from other countries. What's more is that Cuneo and Vaillancourt felt the same way. "And," says Bodine today, "that's how my friends got involved, and to this day, that is how they claim that I ruined all of their lives."

Vaillancourt's and Cuneo's sixth sense about Bodine's idea also stemmed from the fact that they were all car and sports geeks. "Geoff is curious; he is a guy who likes sports technology," says Cuneo. "We figured that given what Geoff had said up in Lake Placid, he had been stewing about it and finally had come to a decision."

Speaking of coming to a decision, Vaillancourt and Cuneo immediately agreed to take on the project, although the only bobsleds they had ever seen were the same ones everyone else saw every four years on Olympic broadcasts, rocketing down remote mountains in snowy locales to the voice of John Morgan. The Bo-Dyn partnership was officially rekindled.

In retrospect, it's probably a good thing that Bodine, Cuneo, and Vaillancourt didn't know much about the sport of bobsledding, or else they may have never gotten past that first telephone conversation. After all, a litany of attempts had been made through the years at rebooting the American bobsled. In addition to the General Motors attempt in the mid-1960s mentioned in Chapter 1, General Electric and Union College made a spirited attempt before the 1980 Lake Placid Games with their flexible, one-piece chassis, with the lead designer boasting that in a few years the sled would "hold most of the records in the world." Needless to say, that prediction didn't exactly come to pass.

Indeed, no single entity had a monopoly on attempts to improve the American bobsled. During the same time period as the General Electric-Union College joint effort, the Excalibur Auto Corporation of Milwaukee patented a newfangled bobsled steering system that the company claimed would win a medal at the Lake Placid Games. One afternoon in March 1979, various U.S. bobsled pilots took the Excalibur sled down the Lake Placid track at Mt. Van Hoevenberg. Excalibur officials quickly squirreled it away in a truck to stop any prying eyes. That effort, too, came to nothing in the end.

Still another company that got into the act was Lederle Laboratories, a pharmaceutical company then based in Pearl River, New York, a sponsor of the 1984 Winter Games. The designer was a man named Bob Said, a former bobsled driver in the 1968 and 1972 Games; whose son Boris was a NASCAR road racing specialist driver, would later become involved in the Bo-Dyn Bobsled Project. The futuristic design looked like it was built "for space travel," according to Morgan, but couldn't make it down the Lake Placid track without almost killing its occupants.

Another outfit that tried to get into the bobsled business was called Air Flow Sciences, which became something of a legendary joke in the mid-1980s. They spent north of $1,000,000 designing a sled and introduced it with great fanfare. It didn't get down the hill within one second of the other sleds, according to Brian Shimer, who started racing in 1985 after a successful college football career. "Anyone who came up in my generation of sliders, we saw plenty of failures when it came to getting an American-designed sled built and be successful," Shimer says.

Tuffy Latour, whose grandfather won the 1959 U.S. bobsled championship with Dew Drop Morgan as his brakeman, started sliding in 1990 after six years in the Air Force. He remembers that when he first came on the scene, a team from Ohio State had bobsled pilots testing sleds the university's Engineering Department had designed. "You had universities and all kinds of groups that tried to build a sled," Latour says. "Even individuals came out of the woodwork." For instance, Latour remembers former Austrian standout, Peter Kienast, who bought two Italian sleds, redid the inner workings, designed new runners, and sold them to the U.S. But when Kienast passed in 1992 after a battle with cancer, the project ended with just the two sleds being refurbished.

It wasn't just the technological or engineering challenges that thwarted these attempts. The dominant mentality surrounding U.S. bobsledding throughout the 1970s and 1980s was an "every man for himself" ethos, due to the chaos that surrounded the financing and availability of sleds.

Every push athlete, every pilot, every team knew that when it came to their equipment, they were on their own. And that encouraged competitiveness and selfishness when it came to the sleds. "Before Bo-Dyn, the mentality seemed like it was every man for himself," says Latour. "You had to find your own sled and somehow buy your own sled. And any person or company that came in and tried to make sleds, they would get frustrated at the process, how there would be all this arguing over who was going to ride what sled, and they would just get frustrated and pull out." In fact, Latour remembers his first thought when he learned of Bodine's pledge to make U.S. sleds that would be provided free of charge to the athletes: the madness surrounding the annual scramble for equipment would finally come to an end. "I was just in my second or third year in the sport, and I think everyone was excited that Geoff made that pledge," Latour says. "It had to be an improvement over what was going on."

Dave Kurtz, the skeleton athlete who had met Geoff Bodine at the Olympic Training Center before Bodine went on his fateful ride with Bruce Roselli, describes those years as marked "by a new guy getting off the bus, saying that he could save U.S. bobsledding." Kurtz says that the major problem was that neither the dysfunctional USBSF Board nor any of the new people coming into the sport in the 1980s had any idea how to get sponsors. "Everyone said they could get sponsors, but no one could do it until Geoff came along, and he got Cuneo to design it; and, because of him, we got major sponsors involved in bobsledding," Kurtz says.

With this litany of previous failures no doubt in mind, members of a temporary bobsled federation came to Cuneo's shop in Oxford, Connecticut to discuss the Bo-Dyn Project. At one point, one of the federation members asked why the Bo-Dyn team believed that it could do what some of the best engineers from the most innovative companies and universities in the world had tried and failed to achieve. "You don't know a damn thing about bobsleds," one of the executives chimed in. "Can you tell us why we should accept help from you?" The answer was left to Bodine, who had the credibility of his 1986 Daytona 500 victory, as well as countless other appearances in the winner's circle, behind him. "It's true; we don't know a damn thing about bobsleds," Bodine said. "But we know a lot about winning."

There are three factors that impact the speed at which a bobsled gets down the hill: the sled itself, the push, and the driver performance. Moreover, what Bodine and Cuneo knew from experience was that knowledge of bobsleds per se wouldn't be as important as a more generalized knowledge of speed. That, in fact, was where many previous attempts at reimagining U.S. bobsledding went wrong. The Excalibur Auto Company's patent from 1983, for example, goes into great detail about its steering mechanism:

"The steering system extends through the front and rear axles, which are coupled to the frame through a suspension system. The cables slide when the steering system is actuated, but are not displaced by movement of their supporting sheaths..."

The description goes on and on like that, oblivious to the fact that in bobsledding, as John Morgan puts it, "It's not the athlete who drives the most; it is the athlete who drives the *least*, who wins the race."

While Excalibur was banking their revolutionary sled on a specific, patented steering system, Cuneo and his team knew that there is rarely a "silver bullet" solution to the problem of how to gain speed After all, bobsledding is a sport, from a technical design point of view, that doesn't make a whole lot of sense. As Frank Briglia, one of Cuneo's most important Bo-Dyn team members who went on to become the long-time mechanic for the U.S. bobsled team puts it: "You can't count on what a sled is going to do because horsepower doesn't play into it. It's a gravity sport. It has a lot to do with how the sled takes the pressure. And of course, every track is different."

Improving performance in bobsledding, then, is as much art as science, and Cuneo was a legendary artist in the garage. He took a holistic approach, starting with the intense feel a bobsled pilot must acquire for the sled. Although bobsleds don't operate the same as race cars – bobsleds don't have engines, don't use brakes going down the track, and only have gravity to help them gain speed – the sports do have interesting similarities. Sleds employ different runners for different tracks just like race cars have different tires for different tracks; no two bobsled runs are identical, just as no two NASCAR setups are the same; and bobsled aerodynamics are wind-tunnel tested, just like stock cars. This constant variability means that bobsled drivers and race cars drivers face similar dilemmas as their environments change. "The challenges with car racing and bobsledding are the same," Cuneo says. "With all the variable conditions, the driver has to feel his sled from his ass to his hands. While the solutions may be totally different, the issues of going faster are the same."

Aerodynamics? Crucial. Material science? Sure, the machine has to be top notch. But to Cuneo and his team, the key to designing a bobsled was the driver feeling like part of one unit with the sled. In fact, whenever U.S. bobsled drivers in the ensuing years would take his or her first ride in a Bo-Dyn sled, the vastly improved bond between sled and driver was what would be noticed first – and that was a big part of what defined Bo-Dyn sleds as "NASCAR" sleds.

For his part, Cuneo today freely admits that there were far more erudite engineers that tried to crack the U.S. bobsled nut. All Cuneo had ever wanted to do was build race cars, and even though his father convinced him to go to college rather than approach cars through the limited lens of a mechanic, he was always more interested in the actual machinery than in any particular engineering philosophy or school of thought. As soon as he could, he signed on with Bob Sharp Racing (the Datsun factory team), where he starting building cars for Bob Sharp and Paul Newman, among others.

"If you put me up against those guys at G.E. who worked with Union College, they would blow me out of the water with their theoretical knowledge," Cuneo says. "But building a winner isn't about theoretical knowledge. It's about applying what you know to the problems a driver faces in going faster."

One would think that the members of the temporary bobsled federation would have been absolutely thrilled that

Bodine was both bringing publicity to the sport through his involvement, as well as engaging one of the top race car designers in the United States to build the sleds — especially since the U.S. national bobsled program was in pretty bad financial straits at the time. "You know, when I was there in Lake Placid, everyone was smiling, shaking my hand," Bodine says. "I had no idea how it all worked. I thought the USOC just paid for everything and that it was all hunky dory."

Bodine and the other members of the Bo-Dyn Project also figured that as soon as the sport's officials heard that racing great Geoff Bodine was going to get involved in bobsledding, they would give the new project funding through grants or whatever financial mechanism that they used. They figured wrong. The officials made it clear that if they wanted to help the U.S. bobsled team, it would be on their dime. "We'll tell you what you need to do," one of the officials told the Bo-Dyn team. "You need to build one and prove that it works." If the Bo-Dyn Project could build one and make it work, then the federation would talk again.

To complicate things, the Olympic cycle was in the midst of a major change. The International Olympic Committee (IOC) had decided to start alternating the Summer Olympics and Winter Games. The plan was to stage a Winter

Olympics competition in Lillehammer, Norway in 1994 – just two years removed from Albertville — to get the Winter Games rebooted on a different four-year cycle than the Summer Games. That way, television would have an Olympics to show every two years. What this meant for the Bo-Dyn Project, however, was that instead of having four years to build a bobsled that would be ready for the next Olympics, Bodine and the Chassis Dynamics crew had just two years.

Despite the time pressure and their inexperience in the sport, the team was determined not to copy previous designs. The initial budget put together by Cuneo and Vaillancourt called for $25,000. That seemed like plenty; after all, how complicated could it be? "The truth is we had no idea what was in those sleds," Bodine says. "For all we knew, they might have been just like those soapbox derby models the Boy Scouts build."

Cuneo and Vaillancourt wanted to get their hands on all the sleds they could: different makes, different brands, different models manufactured in different countries. But, unfortunately, the available menu of sleds they could examine was severely limited. Members of the U.S. bobsled team weren't exactly knocking down the front door of Chassis

Dynamics to offer their sleds for inspection. "Ninety percent of them didn't want anything to do with us," Cuneo says. "The drivers, in particular, wouldn't buy in at first." But among the top drivers (Latour was still relatively new at this point) there was one notable exception – Shimer, who to that point had been on both the 1988 teams and 1992 Olympic teams. Shimer would go on to play an important role in both the Bo-Dyn Project and U.S. bobsledding in general. In fact, even Shimer's very presence in the sport in 1992 marked a big change in U.S. bobsledding, and understanding where his career intersects with the Bo-Dyn Project is crucial to understanding its early days.

Shimer arrived on the Morehead State University campus in Kentucky in 1980, the year after famed quarterback Phil Simms left for the NFL's New York Giants. A running back, Shimer had been All-State in football and was also a star on the baseball and track teams in Naples, Florida, about as far away from the frozen tundra of Lake Placid as it gets. After graduating from Morehead State in 1985, Shimer stayed around campus that summer to start pursuing a teaching certificate with the idea of coaching and teaching high school.

By the time Shimer graduated from Morehead State, though, the USBSF was starting to recruit at colleges and AAU track clubs. Morgan had become executive director of U.S. bobsledding in 1985 and set out to attract better athletes to the sport. For decades, the phrase "bobsledding recruiting" was an oxymoron, with North America's only track tucked away in the northern reaches of upstate New York. It simply wasn't easy to get elite athletes exposed to the sport. This was before the Internet, of course, before the average person had an extremely powerful computer right in their pocket and could Google "bobsledding" and find out everything there is to know about the sport. "At that time," Morgan says, "If you weighed 260 pounds, owned your own sled, and lived close enough to Mount Van Hoevenberg that you could train there, you'd probably be on the Olympic team. I wanted to get drivers who could push sleds so we could compete with the Europeans."

As Shimer puts it today: "Basically, guys who knew bobsledding would be having a beer with some other guys and say, 'Hey, you want to take a ride tomorrow?' That's more or less how people were recruited."

To help him and others determine which athletes had the raw material to meet the new high standards, Morgan and others devised an eight-point test measuring athletic speed, power, and agility (by the time Steve Holcomb came to the sports about 10 years later, the eight-point test had been condensed to a six-point test). Besides writing directly to college athletic departments inquiring about athletes who might be interested, Morgan would also place ads in track and field news and other publications to find potential athletes.

In fact, Morgan's search for athletes knew no bounds. In May 1985 he finagled an infield pass to the NCAA track and field championships in Indianapolis. After the 100 meter and 200 meter trials, Morgan approached the sprinters who were eliminated in the first heat. He'd introduce himself and then casually say something along the lines of, "Hey, you know you're not fast enough to make the US Olympic Track Team, but you might be able to make the U.S. Olympic bobsled team." His presence eventually drew the interest of Larry Ellis, the legendary Princeton track coach and Olympic men's track coach, who had once been Bob Beamon's track coach in high school. Ellis asked Morgan what he was doing. Morgan told him with no hesitation that he was recruiting bobsledding athletes. As Ellis chased him off the infield, the last words Morgan remembered were, "Get the hell off my infield!"

Despite his reception at the 1985 track championships, Morgan hit pay dirt in 1985 with a recruiting class that included Shimer, Roselli, Scott Pladel, and Harvard track star, Jim Herberich. After he had completed his football career, Shimer filled out a questionnaire and took Morgan's eight-point athletic skills test in the presence of a Morehead State track coach, who took down his scores and sent them to U.S. bobsled officials. Morehead's sports information director told Morgan of Shimer's athleticism and that he had won the high school state wrestling championship, in addition to his football heroics. To Shimer's surprise, a plane ticket to Lake Placid arrived in the mail (courtesy of Morgan, who had to pull it out of a petty cash fund, as he knew no one would approve it) for a formal try out. "I figured I had nothing to lose," Shimer says. "It's not like I had these big expectations around bobsledding. I'd barely seen a snowflake in person my entire life."

Shimer sized up the competition at his tryout in Lake Placid and quickly realized he had a chance to make the team. Pilots generally emerge from the existing corps of push athletes, so Shimer wasn't trying to make the U.S. Bobsled team as a pilot. What he needed to do was to push a hell of a last faster than the other guys at the tryout, as the coaches were picking three athletes. They weren't even going down the track, as the Lake Placid track – the only one in North America at the time (the Calgary track was in the process of being built for the 1998 Winter Games) – wouldn't be open for another six weeks or so. "Some of the guys there were not elite athletes; they did not have a lot of strength and speed," Shimer says. "Again, you had the recruiting issue. Essentially, they were local guys who were interested in bobsledding." With his football and track and field background, Shimer, as it turned out, was one of the fastest sprinters and strongest pushers.

Two months later, having made the squad without so much as ever making one run on a bobsled, Shimer found himself on a beautiful mid-November day in Winterberg, Germany, at the top of a bobsled run, staring down the icy track. Down he went, the G-forces pulling him and the speeds intoxicating him. "I remember thinking that this was just so cool," Shimer says. "I had never been a person who necessarily had that 'need for speed' type mindset. I guess I hadn't realized it before."

Hooked on the sport, Shimer had a great time the rest of that week; that is until he experienced his first crash right at the end of the training period. In a matter of seconds, what had seemed like a thrilling, fun week discovering his inner daredevil had turned into a deadly serious business. "I was pretty sure I didn't want to die on the ice 5,000 miles from home," Shimer said. "From that point on, I always took it very seriously and gained a lot of respect for the sport."

By the time the Bo-Dyn Project had begun in earnest, Shimer, along with his USA teammates, had spent the first seven years of his bobsled career using the kind of recycled European sleds that inspired Bodine to launch the project. For example, Matt Roy, the pilot of USA-1 in both the 2-man and the 4-man for most of the mid-to late-1980s, raced a sled that had been owned by Swiss ace pilot Hans Hiltebrand.

How did he come to purchase it? At the time, all Olympic teams were allowed to bring three 2- and 4-man teams to the Games but, after the Wednesday of the training week, had to pick two for the actual competition. Hans Hiltebrand of Switzerland lost the race-off in the 4-man competition at the 1984 Games; and, subsequently, the sled was bought by American business executive, Robert Landau. Landau offered it to U.S. pilot Jeff Jost, who after just two practice runs with the sled, finished 5th — a superhuman effort when you consider he was placing 12th -15th in practice with his old, second-hand 4-man sled. Matt Roy ended up inheriting that sled and used it for several years. "You know, the problem with the way things were back then (and Geoff Bodine was exactly right about this) is that when the Swiss or whoever sold you a sled, they were not selling you something that you were going to beat them with," Shimer says. Indeed, whenever the U.S. would buy one of these castoff sleds, according to both Shimer and Latour, they'd notice the Europeans would, in short order, show up at the next competition with newly designed sleds.

So, going into the Calgary Games in 1988, the U.S. had some decent push athletes, but average equipment, at best, and pilots who were a liability when it came to pushing at the start. Shimer, as the brakeman for both Roy's 2- and 4-mans sled in Calgary, finished in double-digit results in both events. The other 4-man USA sled, driven by Brent Rushlaw of Saranac Lake, New York, just missed a bronze by .02 of a second in a weather-impaired race that was probably more famous for the appearance and crash of the Jamaican bobsled team. Four-time Olympian Rushlaw was a bobsledding throwback who wasn't much into off-season training — which didn't help his lackluster starts — but he was a pure driver who had an amazing feel for getting a European-bought sled down a track.

Shimer flew directly to Lake Placid after the Olympics and got in the front seat of a sled, starting from halfway down the track. "The fire had been lit inside me," Shimer says. "After three years of riding, I wanted to get in that front seat."

Shimer became the pilot of USA-1 in the 2-man, not because of his driving skills, but because his athleticism enabled him to do so well at the start that the competition couldn't quite make up enough time to catch him. Soon he started piloting a 4-man sled as well.

Although Shimer was part of the 1992 Olympic squad in Albertville whose 7th place performance motivated Bodine to vow to build American-made sleds, the irony was that even while the Bo-Dyn Project was gaining traction, Shimer was having a great 1992-1993 season as a result of his athleticism at the start, as well as the recruitment of Herschel Walker, Willie Gault, and Edwin Moses to be his push athletes. The Americans now had the athletes to compete with the Europeans. Shimer won the first three races of the season in the 4-man in a brand new Italian sled, including at Altenburg in Germany, a track known as the one of the world's most difficult, where he set the track record.

Meanwhile, in December 1992, the very first Bo-Dyn sled was being tested by Bruce Rosselli. With very little to go on, Cuneo's shop had designed a prototype that was finished in December 1992, just ten months after the Albertville Games. That first 2-man sled is one that today, in 2016, Bodine is personally restoring as a pet project. "It was beautiful," Bodine says. Not only was the first Bo-Dyn sled nice to look at, but it also went down the mountain in Lake Placid pretty good, as well. But it certainly wasn't ready for prime time yet. "You know, at that point, we didn't know much about the sport; and, of course, we had no information from race results, which is where you get your best data," Cuneo says. That winter of 1993 in Innsbruck, Shimer won the first World Championship medal for the U.S. of any kind since 1967 when he won the bronze in the 4-man competition. "I was really excited about that," Shimer says, "because now Cuneo could see the sled we just won the World Cup with and learn from that as well."

With all of his experience and drive, Shimer was an apt pupil when he arrived in Oxford, Connecticut to sit down with Cuneo and Vaillancourt to further develop the prototype that had already been produced. Again, this was a NASCAR, driver-centric philosophy: Shimer, the racer – not the technology, not the designer, not the manufacturer, not the governing body – was at the center of everyone's focus. "We were going to make our own technology around our drivers and see if it could work," Cuneo says.

Shimer brought two sleds with him. One was an Italian sled he had used at various points in his career, and one was a Swiss-made sled that he had purchased on the spot after a race from a Swiss driver, much like Jeff Jost's transaction with Hans Hildebrand.

The Italian sled was one designed by Sergio Siorpaes, a former Italian bobsled brakeman and the grandson of a famous 19th-century mountaineer, Santo Siorpaes. Sergio Siorpaes won two bronze medals in the 1964 Games with the legendary Eugenio Monti, the Italian bobsled great who won 10 World Cup medals and six Olympic medals, and whose dominance was so great that he is still known as the "Pele" of his sport.

After retiring from competition, Siorapes learned the bobsled building trade from d'Andrea Podar, a sled designer in Cortina who sold some sleds to USA athletes in the late 1960s and 1970s. Siorapes, much like Podar, was basically a blacksmith who started building his own sleds. Not surprisingly, given the sled's age and the modest technology available to Siorapes, the Italian sled was not sleek. "I mean, this thing was old when I first got it," Shimer says. "I remember hearing that he built it in his house." In fact, Siorpaes had a shop next to his house.

The Swiss sled had a much more traditional provenance. At the 1989 World Championships in Cortina Italy, Shimer adapted Jost's method of making an impulse buy right on the mountain. Shimer asked a Swiss driver who had finished behind Matt Roy of the U.S. if he wanted to sell his sled. The pilot, Nico Baracchi, was at first puzzled at the brazenness of Shimer's request. Finally, he responded, "Yeah, if I can't beat USA-1, I'm going to build a better one next year,' so he sold it to me," Shimer recalls.

Six years old at the time of the sale, the sled was still a pretty decent piece of equipment, and Shimer would use it in competition until he started driving Bo-Dyn sleds in 1993. But the Swiss sled came at a steep price for Shimer, both literally and figuratively. Baracchi wanted $20,000 for the sled, with Shimer also paying for the shipping from the mountain. With athletes responsible for their own sleds, Shimer accepted the terms and then spent months fruitlessly promoting himself back in Naples, Florida, as the area's first Winter Olympic athlete. His efforts, for the longest time, were met with curious shrugs, South Florida not being a winter sports hotbed.

After several months, Baracchi was threatening to take the sled back if Shimer couldn't come up with the money. That's when Shimer's parents stepped up and took out a second mortgage. Unfortunately, this was the kind of all-too-common financial hardship that bobsled athletes had to undergo in their sport. The life of bobsled athletes was not – and certainly isn't today — akin to the life of famous Olympics skiers such as Bode Miller or Lindsey Vonn, household names who make millions in endorsement contracts. It's the sexy commercial sports like figure staking and downhill skiing that get the resources and the big sponsorships because companies want to sell skates and skis. There aren't too many American families in the market for a bobsled. "No one's going to run out and buy a bobsled because they see Steve Holcomb racing it," says Shimer.

With both sleds safely in Cuneo's garage, Cuneo and Vaillancourt went to work. Unlike the bobsled bodies today, which can be removed, back in 1993, the bodies didn't come off unless someone ripped them off. Once the team took the sleds apart, they realized that the mechanisms were quite a bit more complicated than they had anticipated. The workings underneath the body were complex and required a lot of technical knowledge to understand exactly what was going on, even for a bunch of self-proclaimed gearheads who had spent decades looking under the hoods of highly temperamental race cars.

Instead of simple frame rails with a little steering mechanism hooked in, the sleds had front and back pivots that rotated to control the "articulation" – that is, how the front and back of the sleds worked together — so that when the sled came off a corner, it wouldn't be such a rough ride for the driver. Grudgingly impressed, Cuneo and Vaillancourt called up Bodine and delivered the news: first of all, the bobsleds were unexpectedly intricate. Second, if they were to build a machine along these lines – only a lot better, of course — they were going to need more money

Given that the Bo-Dyn team all grew up around race cars, the team also thought it crucial to improve the aesthetics. The European designers had never really spent time on the sleekness, the paint job, the overall competitive vibe given off. "Since a lot of these things were old castoffs, that area needed a lot of work," Bodine says. "And I knew Bob and Bobby could totally transform the sleds in that area. The main message from them was that they wanted to do the project, but that these sleds were entirely something else than what we expected, and it was going to take a lot more effort than anyone thought."

As the Chassis Dynamics team stripped the sleds down, Shimer enjoyed an unexpected bonus. Certain parts on his Swiss sled were wearing down now that it was pushing ten years old. It had already been weighing on Shimer's mind that he had to make improvements for the next season. As the rapid-fire nature of Cuneo and Vaillancourt's diagnosis of how the sleds could be improved progressed, their sessions resulted in real-time improvements for his Swiss sled, not just for some unrealized future Bo-Dyn sled. "It was like I was getting a master class not only in bobsled design but also how I could improve the sled that I already had," Shimer says. "They were stripping the thing down and helping me refurbish it, and, at the same time, they were benefiting because they could see how a Swiss sled was built, how an Italian sled was built, and how they compared."

They asked Shimer a million questions centered on what he liked and didn't like about the designs. "We asked him what he thought was needed that he didn't have," Cuneo says. "If he woke up to his dream sled, what would it look like? How would it handle?" The questions kept coming: Did he like this kind of steering? What about the shape of the sled? How did the two sleds handle differently?

A few days turned into a few weeks, and before he knew it, Shimer had spent most of the summer of 1993 there in Oxford, staying with a friend of Cuneo's. Through that experience, Shimer for the first time understood what made a bobsled tick and how an excellent design team approached improving performance. "That's the first time I thought to myself, 'Wow, with the seriousness and professionalism that these guys are bringing to this, I'll do whatever it takes to get better.' I couldn't wait to get started taking the improvements to the track."

In what would become a refrain for scores of U.S. bobsled pilots over the next decade and a half, it was the Bo-Dyn team's attention to detail – those NASCAR intangibles that connect the machines to the driver – that impressed Shimer most. "I would have never thought of all the little things they thought of to improve my sled," Shimer says. "Already, even though they hadn't built a single sled, it was clear how the race car industry predicated everything they did. When you build race cars, everything is so meticulous and precise and clean. Taking pride in the way it looks and just not cutting corners."

Besides Shimer's sleds, there was another important 2-man design that influenced Bodine, Cuneo, and Vaillancourt. This was a sled built by a California-based engineer and bobsled pilot named Brian Richardson, who had a mechanical engineering degree from University of California at Berkeley. Richardson wasn't much of an athlete, but he did make the Albertville Olympic team with his own unusually designed sled. His push start to race was typically abysmal no matter how fast or athletic his brakeman was; to Shimer, it sometimes appeared as if Richardson was walking down the track before jumping into his sled. Richardson was also someone who knew his limitations. In an interview in 2014 with his hometown *San Jose Mercury News*, Richardson recalled his bobsledding ability this way: "I was relatively small for the sport and not very fast. Most people thought I was nuts, and it was a real long shot for me to make the 1992 Olympic team."

But Richardson shocked everyone when he finished second behind Shimer in the 2-man Olympic trials, staged on the old track in Lake Placid in March 1991. Richardson and his brakeman, Greg Harrel, formerly of the Oakland Raiders, faced a huge time deficit. "They were just getting destroyed at the start, but Richardson would make it up on the way down because of the sled," Shimer says. The time made up on the way down the track was so unbelievable that many watching thought that Richardson had some kind of timing mechanism built into the sled that was affecting the track clocks. But no one could prove a thing. "He was starting something like 40/100ths behind Shimer, and then wins in the end," Morgan says. "Everyone was speechless."

Richardson's innovation came in reducing the aerodynamic drag caused by the cowling, or hull, of the sled. Cowlings, by bobsled rules, have to be a specific width and height. Richardson changed the shape of the cowling to reduce the cross-sectional area, thereby cutting down on the drag. The changes Richardson introduced made the final shape of his sled appear to have airplane wings. According to Shimer, Richardson's sled was not the first bobsled design to create this effect; the Swiss, years earlier, also had a line of sleds that peaked out on the sides and angled back in at the bottom, similar to Richardson's. Richardson went on to finish 24th at the 1992 Olympic Games, proving how important the 50m start was in bobsledding.

While Richardson's cowling soon became illegal after some rule changes, Cuneo and Vaillancourt looked at this sled with its unusual cowling and knew it had to be fast. They adapted it to a legal design, and that shape became the basis for the future Bo-Dyn sleds. "The Bo-Dyn sleds never lost that shape, all the way up through the Night Train," Shimer says.

In those early days, Bodine was often present with the Chassis Dynamics team. In fact, Bodine, Cuneo, and Vaillancourt sometimes spent days together at a time. In many ways, the project was a lifeline for Bodine as wins on the race car track came few and far between, and he suffered setbacks in his personal life. "In the very beginning Geoff was around every day," Cuneo says. "He was there for us all the time. There came a point where Geoff's career was in jeopardy. He went through a divorce; he had business problems. He became very involved emotionally with this project."

In that way, Bodine was no different than any of the other members of the Bo-Dyn Project. What he had started with a simple observation in the winter of 1992 was now a mission for a group of designers and builders who could already see their vision becoming a reality. They had developed a prototype sled that could get down a track, yes, and they had imagined a NASCAR sled. Now they had to build it.

Chapter Three

The Making of a NASCAR Sled

AS THE BO-DYN team operated its "skunk works" with Shimer in Connecticut, the suits at the USBSF in Lake Placid grew more and more worried. There's a common term that's become ubiquitous in 2017 to describe everything from augmented reality goggles to driverless cars: "disruptor." Any phenomenon that challenges the old order — be it a company, a person, consumer behavior or cultural shift — is labeled a disruptor. Well, that particular usage of the word "disruptor" wasn't in common parlance in the early 1990s, but Geoff Bodine and the Bo-Dyn Project were classic disruptors, and the primary *disruptees* was the USA Bobsled Board of Directors.

Even as Bodine was pouring money into the project —
he spent about $150,000 of his own money between the 1992
Albertville Games and the 1994 Lillehammer Games when the
first fleet of Bo-Dyn sleds was introduced into competition — a
new USA Bobsled Board was finally elected in 1993,
rebranding itself as the USBSF and replacing the interim
Board. But they didn't know the sport, and most of them
attended no races and made little effort to get to know the
athletes. The pattern for the USBSF — which would essentially
continue throughout the Bo-Dyn era — was that a Board
would be in place for one or two Olympics before being
overhauled due to retirements and or elections. As John
Morgan likes to say about what he's seen in a long career
spent in virtually every nook and cranny of bobsledding: "I
have learned that the only thing amateur about amateur
sports is the people who run them."

"Yeah, they put up a lot of walls," Bodine says. "Once
they realized that, 'Boy, this guy is serious about this, and he
is going to challenge us, and we're going to lose all this stuff,'
they were not very receptive to us."

By the autumn of 1993, based on their
experimentation with Shimer's sleds and the Richardson sled
— as well as in looking at how the prototype sled had tested

with Bruce Rosselli — Cuneo and Vaillancourt had some ideas for Bodine about what direction they wanted to take the 2-man sled. Initially, much of the focus was on making the articulation just so, as Cuneo believed the pilots needed superb "feel" for the sled. In terms of specific areas of improvement, the first big one was the cowling and the shape, based on the Richardson sled, to improve aerodynamics. Other changes were planned for what's called the torsion bar, improvements to which would make the sled much more adjustable based on the conditions. A third adaption was with the steering, which they wanted to make more responsive.

As for materials, the team was committed to only the highest-quality, lightweight aluminum and high-tech alloys so that the sled's weight could be distributed in all four corners of the vehicle, similar to how weight is distributed in auto racing. Most important, the team knew that it wanted a sled that could be fine-tuned, just like the race cars they worked on. It had to be able to be broken down quickly into its components so that new components could be added and the suspension and steering tweaked, depending on the individual track.

Then there was the question of process. How would the team work together to design the sled? Chassis Dynamics often worked with a mechanical design company, Creative Product Development, located right next door and owned and operated by a long-time friend, Don Barker. Barker had a computer system for which he designed all kinds of industrial equipment, and there was no reason it couldn't be used to design a bobsled. While computer design programs have come a long way in the last 25 years, what could be done digitally in 1993 was still an enormous improvement over manually plugging in figures and dimensions to create a model. "That's how they designed the model of the sled; Don and his company were invaluable," Bodine says.

In fact, the Bo-Dyn Project was the first bobsled design effort to use computer-aided design, already standard in the car racing business in the early 1990s. In simple terms, it would allow Cuneo's team to be far more productive by replacing hard copy drawings and designs with design software. Using computer-assisted design, Cuneo could model different designs all on a computer. Three-dimensional digital mock-ups were created that Bodine could check out before Cuneo and Vaillancourt physically built anything.

Computer-generated simulations would allow the team to estimate air flow over the body of the sleds, depending on the materials used for the sled. Plug in a material with a different weight and the aerodynamic difference could be seen right there on the computer screen. With this methodology, the team hoped to produce a fleet of sleds in time for Lillehammer, a feat that even some on the project thought would be a tall order. "When you look at where they were starting, and what they had to do, you might think it would take three or four years, and they had about 18 months," Shimer says.

Soon, Cuneo had a design for the chassis, and once Cuneo had the frame set on the fixture, it was Frank Briglia's turn. Whenever it was time to *really* get to work at Chassis Dynamics, it meant that Briglia could not be far away. By 1993, Briglia had known Cuneo for more than 20 years, building fiberglass parts, molds, and bodies for the cars that Cuneo designed and built in his shop. Briglia was a savvy businessman as well. As a fiberglass man at heart, he realized that boaters could use his skills as well, so he had opened a boat repair shop in Wolcott, conveniently just a short drive from Cuneo's shop. While fiberglass boat repair on sailboats, pleasure craft, big motor boats – whatever cruised in over the transom – was Briglia's day job, his passion, not surprisingly, was cars.

"I'm self-taught in everything I've done," he says. "I've been playing with cars since I was 15 years old. Cars were always my thing, like everyone else who got involved in the Bo-Dyn Project."

It was Briglia's job to take the chassis design and make the fiberglass mold for the cowling. After that, other members of Cuneo's team would make the parts, fit them, and mount the steel to the frame. "Once we needed Frank's fiberglass skills, there was a lot of back and forth at each other's shops," Cuneo says. "Especially with the way people in this business drive, a 20-minute drive for most normal people doesn't take quite as long for one of us." Soon enough, it was clear that Briglia was set on making his contribution to the sled his finest work to date. He experimented with various composites for the body, and the final product was something that even years later when major companies were trying to copy Bo-Dyn sleds, they couldn't come up with a better composite for the body.

Besides Briglia, Cuneo, and Vaillancourt had a wealth of other talent to choose from. Connecticut's auto racing tradition and many fine tracks had encouraged a whole generation of mechanics, welders, body men, retouching experts, and painters. Angelo Guerrera and Tommy Centenaro, for example, worked on the body of the sleds and, later, the painting. Guerrera's specific area of expertise was the shaping of the body, and he became such an expert on the Bo-Dyn sleds that each summer until 2011, in fact, he rebuilt the sleds to get them ready for the next World Cup season.

Throughout this entire design period, Bodine was holding firm that every bolt, screw, and joint on the sleds must be made in the U.S. But a snafu in the team's "Made in America" credo soon cropped up. A bobsled's runners are the two sets of blades on the bottom of the sled that run on the track. Cuneo and Vaillancourt soon found that there was no American company that made the right kind of steel for the runners. So the team had to use a type of Austrian steel famous for forging small-to-medium sized tools. It was a tough conversation to have with Bodine, but everyone agreed that they had done everything they could to make every part a U.S.-made piece of equipment. If the steel couldn't be American, Cuneo decided to do the next best thing. At least the steel could be milled and cut in the U.S., which it was, at the Maho Machine Tool Corporation in Naugatuck, Connecticut.

While wind testing was fairly common in bobsledding, Bo-Dyn brought it to the next level. Having been steeped in race car culture, Bodine, Cuneo and Vaillancourt understood how testing under various scenarios could provide clues to how the sleds would respond in much different conditions. Wind tunnel testing pushes air past a stationary vehicle in a controlled environment, enabling a design team to test the aerodynamics. The first wind tunnel testing for Bo-Dyn sleds took place in Washington State at a Boeing facility, followed by testing at facilities in Maryland and North Carolina. The testing gave the team at Chassis Dynamics more information as they tried different accouterments and parts, even down to the colored decals that were put on the sled.

"You get so much information from wind testing; you literally can go through and make these small adjustments, and it really affects the aerodynamics," Briglia says. Cuneo and Briglia remember one time when, in an attempt to see just how much drag a team could eliminate in total, the Bo-Dyn engineers ordered an entire 4-man team – pilot and the three push athletes – to strip down to their boxers. "I'm not sure why we don't have a picture of that," Cuneo jokes.

One thing always on the minds of the Bo-Dyn team was the ticking clock. In the spring of 1993, they had under a year to build a fleet of these sleds. Cuneo and Vaillancourt put everything else on hold to work on the Bo-Dyn sleds. Angelo Guerrera remembers a pattern of going to Cuneo's shop after his day job on week nights, spending three or four hours with the team, and then coming back on weekends. On Saturday or Sunday nights after working on the sleds, they'd all go down to a local Italian restaurant that many of them still go to today. Guerrera had done numerous projects for Cuneo and loved his creativity and the atmosphere he created at his shop, one in which everyone felt that were all in this fantastic adventure together. "I mean here we were, a bunch of local car nuts, getting to do work for the U.S. Olympic team," Guerrera says "I loved every minute of it."

One late night at the shop, everyone sleep-deprived and woozy from the 24/7 preparations of the sleds for Lillehammer, Briglia started, as a joke, referring to themselves as "Team Provolone," given the Italian roots of several of them. Soon, decals were made for all of the sleds, showing a wheel of cheese with a little slice missing.

What wasn't fun, however, was trying to pay for everything. Big sponsorships were hard to come by, even with Bodine's race cred. Even then, though, there were some companies that were intrigued enough by Bodine's participation, or perhaps knew Cuneo's work from the auto racing circuit, and were interested in being associated with the Bo-Dyn Project. Some of these companies – powder coating companies, nut and bolt companies — were critical in the lean years. "These were unsung people," Cuneo says. "Early on we had a bunch of small sponsors that helped out quite a bit with supplying materials and such."

One aspect of working with the USBSF that continually frustrated the Bo-Dyn team was the fact that the organization insisted that any Bo-Dyn fundraising be reflected in the checking account of the USBSF. While that simply looked like a money grab to the Bo-Dyn team, the reality was more complicated. The USOC allocated their resources to their sports' governing bodies based on two things: results and how well the governing bodies could raise money on their own. In other words, the USOC had little interest in throwing good money after bad; only the successful governing bodies would get significant funding.

Given bobsled's recent history in the U.S., the USBSF wouldn't be getting recognized for results. Therefore, it was desperate to try and get funding based on fundraising. Since the NASCAR-hardened Bo-Dyn was so much better at it and wanted "in" on their sport, the USBSF considered the Bo-Dyn fundraising skills as the price of admission, so to speak. "There were large periods of time when we were raising more money than they were," says Cuneo. "They wanted that money so they could get credit for raising it." The real problem, however, wasn't that the USBSF was greedy or meant to do the Bo-Dyn team harm by taking their money. The issue was that once the money that the Bo-Dyn Project raised found its way into the USBSF coffers, the Board's poor management meant that when a bill came it couldn't pay, or some travel by a coach needed to be paid for, it would dip into the funds that should have been earmarked for Bo-Dyn marketing expenses or equipment. "It wasn't that they were bad people, in my mind," Cuneo says. "But they were horrible managers and terrible with money."

On the other hand, Bodine and Cuneo, both coming from the car racing world — which is all about the sponsorships – knew the levers that had to be pulled and the egos that had to be stroked to land a corporate sponsorship. Years before tennis players and golfers wore caps and shirts plastered with logos; race car drivers were accustomed to serving as walking billboards for national companies and their local greasy spoons alike.

Financially, things started looking up when IBM came aboard as a sponsor, providing computers and some significant funding. How did the team land IBM as an initial sponsor? According to Bodine, it's never been exactly clear who closed the deal. Someone affiliated with the Bo-Dyn Project delivered a message to IBM that Bo-Dyn wasn't just building a sled – they were going over to Lillehammer to win a gold medal. "They said it just like that as if it was going to be a piece of cake," Bodine says. "It wasn't me, or Bob or Bobby. But someone said it, and I guess IBM heard that and liked it." Part of the deal was undoubtedly linked to the fact that IBM was also the official timing sponsor of the 1994 Winter Olympic Games, so for IBM, it may have been a natural fit. "That was huge," Tuffy Latour says. "Just a short time into the project, Geoff's involvement made it a legitimate program by bringing in a major sponsorship, which was unheard of."

With Lillehammer approaching and some funding coming in, it was decided that the core members of the team would test one of the sleds in Lillehammer in March 1993 at the pre-Olympic test, in which the competing nations descend on the Olympic track for a week shortly before the Games and familiarize themselves with the conditions. This being the first of the Bo-Dyn team's many trips to Europe, hijinks ensued almost immediately when the team shipped the sled to Oslo, only to find that its rented van was too small to transport the sled for the four-hour drive to Lillehammer. Try as they might, Vaillancourt, Barker, and Cuneo couldn't fit the crate into what Cuneo calls "that shitty little van they had given us."

So, on a quiet Oslo Sunday morning, with, needless to say, no Norwegian speakers among their group, they set out trying to rent a truck. The young English speakers they found had no idea where they could do such a thing, and the older people they encountered spoke no English, although they did gesticulate wildly. Finally, they found an out-of-the-way establishment that rented boat trailers, and a young man who served as translator. When they brought the trailer back to the airport, however, they had one more challenge: "They wouldn't let us have the sled," Barker says. "Something about not having the right paperwork." Deciding to have dinner and then deal with customs, the boys came back to the airport, only to find the crate unmanned. They backed the boat trailer up, opened the door, tied the sled on with 100 feet of rope that they had also procured at the boat shop, and were off. "After we had tested the sled, I'd say we were a little nervous when it was time to go back through the Oslo airport," Cuneo says.

As far as the actual test, the team was extremely pleased with the results, despite it being declared illegal because of a technicality that was easily addressed back in Cuneo's shop in Oxford. A return trip to Lillehammer was made in October 1993, just a few months before the Games, this time with two IBM computer analysts who were tracking the sleds' "vitals" with their IBM ThinkPad laptops. The information on what the sleds was experiencing – the G-forces, the vibration, the steering, how the sled was articulating – was invaluable to Cuneo. Morgan, who was there, witnessed the very NASCAR-like gathering of precisely what was going on with the sled, and likes to say that it was that day that "the sport of bobsledding entered the 21st century."

By the time the Lillehammer Games came along in February 1994, Cuneo's team had completed three 2-man sleds and three 4-man sleds. At that point, the 4-man sled design wasn't being pursued as a separate design project; Cuneo was more or less copying his innovations from the 2-man sled. This philosophy would later be regarded as a mistake by Cuneo himself, and he would later treat the designs of the two different sleds very differently. In his defense, however, it was a miracle just to have these sleds ready by Lillehammer.

After all, their budget for these two years was about $400,000, for which Bodine provided almost half out of pocket. With that budget, Chassis Dynamics had to pay for R&D, all of the materials, the time for all the people on the project, and all the various incidentals that cropped up. "We had a bunch of chumps in Connecticut called Team Provolone," Cuneo says, referring to his own beloved team. For comparison's sake, the Germans had approximately a $3.8 million budget *just* for R&D during these years.

"I don't want to say it was impossible what Bob (Cuneo) and Bobby (Vaillancourt) did because it happened," Bodine says. "So I'll just say it was absolutely incredible. There's a picture somewhere of all the sleds lined up in front of Cuneo's shop before they went to Europe for the 1994 Olympics. It was unbelievable."

Chapter Four

The Unveiling of a NASCAR Sled

JUST 24 ACTION-PACKED months after Bodine's life changed because of the Albertville Games, the U.S. team showed up in Lillehammer with American-made sleds. Compared to the European sleds the team was using at the time, the sleds were a Godsend. At that point, the athletes were accustomed to using veritable Frankenstein bobsleds, with parts crudely assembled. On these sleds, everything fit together perfectly. The athletes found that they could change a certain bolt out, and the sled would run a little "softer;" put it back in, and it would run a little "stiffer." "That's really the tie into NASCAR," says Latour. "You could run a sled with the same spring setup, the same steering set-up, the same center-rear rubbers, and then the next day Cuneo would say,

'Well, why don't we do this; why don't we do that?' It gave us a different perspective on what to try."

Still, it wasn't clear that all the U.S. competitors would use the sleds. Remember, they had been using European-made sleds all the way through that World Cup season, which was in mid-season. In fact, according to David Kurtz, who by 1993 had retired as a skeleton athlete and was respected enough by the sliding community to be named team captain of the Men's U.S. Bobsled Team, a high U.S. finish in the 1993 World Championships in a non-Bo-Dyn sled fueled some controversy among the athletes about whether the Bo-Dyn sleds should be used in Lillehammer. "You have to remember, up until that point, foreigners had more credibility in the sport than Americans did," Kurtz says. "Most of our coaches had not been born in the U.S., our equipment was made in Europe, and Europeans had dominated the sport for decades. So when Geoff Bodine said he wanted to make American-made sleds, that was great, but it was going against the grain of what had become the norm. There was some skepticism – even among the U.S team – about all the rah-rah American stuff." Kurtz knew that Bo-Dyn sleds were surely the future of American bobsledding given the seriousness with which Bodine, Cuneo, and Vaillancourt were going about their business but didn't feel like he could force the Bo-Dyn sleds on athletes who were already comfortable with their own equipment. "As a team captain, I'm sort of like the general manager," Kurtz says. "And as a skeleton guy, not a bobsled guy, I wasn't comfortable saying, 'Okay, you have to use this particular sled.'"

So, for all those reasons, in addition to the Bo-Dyn sleds, other sleds, like the Italian-made machines that the team had been using the past couple of World Cup seasons, were brought along to Lillehammer as well. Cuneo, Vaillancourt, and Barker went to Lillehammer about ten days early to prepare the sleds, and it was their job to have the Bo-Dyn sleds ready when the American sliders called for them.

In terms of presentation, the sleds weren't all the same red, white, and blue designs. Some had stars and stripes, some had flags, and one particularly memorable sled sported flames on the side panels. "We came out with these beautiful, awesome looking sleds," Bodine says. The Europeans knew that the race car builders were on to something. Even though the first batch of 2-man sleds was not particularly fast relative to what was to come, they had that unique Bo-Dyn look. "They saw it coming," Briglia says. "And the biggest thing I noticed was that the Europeans become a lot friendlier. It's sort of like this: when you're a nobody, nobody wants to talk to you. After those sleds had come out, U.S. athletes weren't nobodies anymore."

As the opposing coaches, athletes, and the media marveled at the workmanship of the U.S. sleds, the question everyone wanted to be answered was: How fast were they?" Not fast enough to win medals so soon after the project started, but fast enough to send the message that the Americans were heading for the summit of Olympic bobsledding.

The results in Lillehammer were held back by the lack of knowledge of the sport. Cuneo and his team didn't know how to tune a sled for a certain track, for example, so hadn't heavily factored in the ins and outs of the Lillehammer track. Like a talented but inexperienced football team playing in its first Super Bowl, "Team Provolone" had made good sleds but wasn't quite ready for such a big stage. Pilots Shimer and Herberich finished 13th and 14th with their 2-man sleds, respectively. In the 4-man, Shimer's sled was disqualified at the start of the second day of competition for "hot runners," as his steel blades at the bottom of the sled didn't meet temperature requirements. Shimer had been a respectable

9th place after the second run. Randy Will, not piloting a Bo-Dyn sled, finished in 15th place.

Despite the final results at Lillehammer, however, the Bo-Dyn Project was starting to inculcate the NASCAR culture of improvisation and experimentation. They had a huge trailer with spare parts and variations on those parts, signaling a new way of doing things — the NASCAR way – in which nothing is ever a finished product. Right from the very beginning, starting in Lillehammer, Cuneo and his team treated the sleds as works in progress, watching to see what made them tick on that particular day and then tweaking them to coax out some more speed.

One incident in Lillehammer is of particular note because it's a perfect embodiment of how the Bo-Dyn Project fostered cooperation as much as competition. Switzerland's Gustav Weder, who would go on to win the 2-man gold later that week, somehow managed to break his sled. Weder, it must be understood, was famously mysterious and reclusive, with no one ever getting a look at his sled before a competition. He came to the Bo-Dyn team for help, hoping against hope that the extra parts and materials the team had brought could be of some use to him. The U.S. had rented a cow barn on a farm to work on the sleds, not far from the cabin where the Bo-Dyn team slept (and where the farmer would come out with something to drink each night, but that's another story). Briglia, Barker, and Cuneo helped fix Weder's sled. He then went out and made history, winning his second consecutive Olympic gold medal in the 2-man.

The consensus among the athletes was that Cuneo and Vaillancourt were close to something big. "It felt great to drive one finally," Shimer says. "It just worked." For Cuneo, Lillehammer was a real watershed because it also came with a Eureka moment. After getting feedback from the team, he tried a change that altered the way the 2-man sleds flexed under pressure at the corners.

One humorous episode in Lillehammer illustrates how the Bo-Dyn engineering innovations were already being noticed and also shows how the national teams both competed — and worked cooperatively with each other — to push the design envelope.

The man in charge of designing Italy's sleds, Diego Menardi, approached Team Provolone member Don Barker during some down time and said how impressed he was with the Bo-Dyn sleds' push bars, which had a unique way of folding up. Barker, being the good sport that he was, sat down with Menardi and drew it out for him. Menardi had more questions. So Barker drew it again. He ended up drawing it "maybe ten times," he says today. Finally, Menardi says, "Well, why don't you just tell me exactly how it works."

At this point, not wanting to give up any trade secrets, Barker went to Cuneo. "Hey," he said. "There's a guy from Italy who wants to know how the push bar works. We don't want to tell him, do we?" Cuneo thought for a moment. "You know, there is something we want from them; I want to know how the rubber works in their runners." Cuneo had been struggling to come up with the exact right composition of rubber for the runners. So a deal was made, and the exchange was made that night – the print-out for the push bar was exchanged for a green material that was a key component in the Italian runners.

The World Cup season after Lillehammer, the 1994-1995 campaign, the Bo-Dyn sleds continued to usher in a new era of bobsledding. The travel schedule was such that Cuneo's team would take turns traveling on the circuit; Cuneo taking two weeks on the road, then Bobby, Frank, and Barker. Whoever was traveling with the team would change the components out every week, sometimes each day between heats. The welders and designers on staff would work all night, cutting and changing things, so the next day, it would essentially be a different sled. "We worked on the fly," Cuneo says. "We'd go to a race and haul everything we might need with us. We'd take the sleds apart every day. Most of the athletes just thought we were pains in the ass."

But Latour probably speaks for many U.S. pilots during that period when he says it was a wonderful new luxury having mechanics with them full-time, listening to what the teams were saying, and employing that race-car mentality to quickly tweak the sleds. "Cuneo, Frank, Don, these were men taking weeks out of their lives, making very little money, to come over to snowy Europe and help out the team," Latour says. "As they learned the sleds, and we learned the sleds, it was only a matter of time before we started to excel."

The biggest challenge to conventional wisdom was when Cuneo & Company would change everything up even when things were going *well*. Not even the European powers like Germany would throw all the pieces up in the air midweek on the World Cup Circuit and see where they landed. Cuneo likens this approach to short track car racing, in which a driver might win a heat to qualify for the main race, and then tinker for an hour before the next. "Everything we were about was never giving up and trying to get more speed to win," Cuneo says. "It didn't matter if we were two-tenths of a second behind or two-tenths of a second ahead after the first heat. The auto racing fraternity is like that, and that's what we decided we had to bring to these sleds."

According to Kurtz, in a sport where the difference between the medal podium and finding another career are decided by just a few hundredths of a second, the American athletes on the circuit didn't take long to embrace Cuneo, Frank Briglia, and the other dedicated Bo-Dyn Project members. "When everyone saw how dedicated they were, how late they were in the garage, how quickly our sleds would bounce back after getting banged up, because of all the replacement parts and such – that NASCAR way of doing things – that's what mentally won over the guys and the coaches."

The World Cup bobsled season runs from December through March, starting in the U.S. and Canada then moving on to Europe for most of the season. Shimer described a scene that was repeated every weekend in the World Cup Circuit starting in the 1994-1995 season. First the sleek, sharp-looking sleds would be unloaded out of the trailer, followed by the trailer filled with bins of spare parts of every imaginable type — parts to replace those that didn't hold up, parts that would dial in the sled differently for different track conditions, bolts needed to put different runners on – the list just goes on and on. It was a show that Shimer never tired of. "To everyone watching it was like, 'Holy shit, these guys just showed up to qualify at Daytona,'" Shimer says with a laugh. "That was the biggest eye-opener. Cuneo and those guys didn't just come with a sled and a wrench. Before Bo-Dyn sleds came along, if we lost a bolt to one of our sleds, we had to find one in the local hardware store; and if you were in the U.S., good luck finding one in metric, because all of our sleds were European built."

It was during this period that the NASCAR mentality started to transform bobsledding not only in the U.S., but worldwide. The bar had been raised from the technical, design, and innovation perspectives. The nations that were bobsled powers, with resources that vastly outgunned the Bo-Dyn Project, would be forced to try to keep pace. After all, if U.S. sleds were adjustable on the fly to gain more speed depending on the track conditions or the weather, drivers from other nations wanted these same advantages. But Cuneo wasn't standing still either. Each race, each season, as the Project evolved, the sleds got faster and faster and that eventually carried into the 4-man sleds, as well. As the team captain, Kurtz had a front-row seat as a witness to the effect that Cuneo and his team were having on U.S. bobsledding.

Soon, though, the travel started to wear on the Bo-Dyn team, and it was clear that the revolving door of traveling mechanics wasn't working; someone had to go on tour full-time. That's when Briglia volunteered. Why? At that point, he knew the most about the upkeep of the sleds. He didn't mind the travel. Also, the idea of a full-time role with U.S. bobsledding appealed to him, as he became an employee of U.S. bobsledding. Lastly, he thought it might be fun.

"And it was fun, but it was a lot of work, too," Briglia says. "Because I was the only one who went with the sleds, I had this large weight I was carrying on my back. I had to keep things running and try to make improvements because we were still looking for more speed."

Regarding feedback from the athletes, after Lillehammer, it wasn't just Shimer contributing anymore. Other pilots wanted to be part of the action now, as well. Latour, in particular, had an epiphany just before that 1994-1995 World Cup season. Latour, who had been sliding for a couple of years at this point, had his first opportunity to drive a Bo-Dyn sled in Calgary while the U.S. team was training for the World Cup circuit. He had seen Bo-Dyn sleds tested in Lake Placid before Lillehammer, but didn't get to try one.

Shimer had his blue Bo-Dyn sled he had raced in Lillehammer, and U.S. pilot, Jim Herberich, had his red sled. Latour, the newcomer, took the new black sled that was put together with some extra parts and was considered too slow for Shimer or Herberich. It shot down the mountain. "I was flying in this Bo-Dyn sled," Latour says. "It was supposedly a lot slower than the blue and the red one, and Cuneo didn't know what to think. It wasn't too long after that Brian took that sled from me," Latour says with a chuckle.

Latour's first time down the hill with a Bo-Dyn sled is instructive for a couple of reasons. Already, in one run, the steering system blew Latour way. According to him, even though he had never been in a race car, it handled as he imagined a race car must feel when it's calibrated perfectly for the driver. "I can still remember jumping in that day in Calgary and driving it and thinking that this was unlike any other sled I'd ever driven in my life," Latour says. "It was so responsive, and it went right where I wanted it to go. The steering system, I'd say, is one of the most innovative things that Cuneo and Geoff did." It made sense that the steering was a differentiator, as Cuneo and Bodine had worked together in designing a unique power steering system for Geoff Bodine's 1986 Daytona win.

Shimer also remembers that day and how this greenhorn, Latour, kept getting the best of him. "Tuffy's a pretty new pilot at that point; you have to remember," Shimer says. "And even though I'm beating him at the start, he's clearly going faster than me. And I'm thinking, 'What the heck is going on?'"

Since Shimer won the team trials in Calgary in November 1994, he had the first pick of equipment. Before he took the faster sled, he asked Cuneo if he could adjust his sled to perform like Latour's, but Cuneo said that was one change that couldn't be done on the road. Shimer looked at his teammate and said, "I'm sorry Tuffy, but I have to take that sled." Soon after, that sled earned its first World Cup medal.

More importantly, though, that unexpected performance from the black sled began a period of Cuneo-driven experimentation in which Latour, Shimer, and Herberich were all involved. Working with Cuneo, the three drivers shared information on sled performance, borrowed each other's runners, and took turns on different sleds. For Cuneo, it was a mountain of anecdotal data that was precious, supercharging the design process and fostering innovation. For Latour, it was a time he remembers as pure bobsledding heaven. "Everybody worked together and tried to get better each and every day in training," Latour says. "That period, from sort of '94 over the next couple of years, was one of the most fun times in my sliding career. Brian, Jim, and I worked together to make the sleds go faster, and then on race day in the World Cup or whatever, it was just let the best man win."

Briglia also noticed that any tensions within the top U.S. drivers disappeared and a real camaraderie formed. "Before it seemed everyone was separate; there was some backbiting," Briglia says. "But when we got involved with these three guys, it was just great." As the walls came down, the working relationships between designers and drivers got more and more informal. Latour and Shimer would try a tweak, and then call Cuneo and let him know what happened, and whether or not it worked. "We started gaining speed with all of this experimentation going on, and it was just great," Latour says.

Of course, not everything fell into place after Lillehammer. Partly from being different, partly because it took a while to get results, and perhaps partly due to some fear and jealousy, the Bo-Dyn Project became a punch line to some. At a team captains' meeting in 1994, Swiss and German athletes were having a good laugh at the expense of some of the recent results of the Bo-Dyn sleds. "We were a laughingstock to some people, because here we showed up with all of our equipment, had these beautiful machines, and weren't getting the results right away," Cuneo says. At that team captains' meeting, a Swiss racer, the former three-time world champion Hans Hildebrand, interrupted the fun. "Don't laugh at them," Hildebrand said to the other Europeans. "I am watching them. In a couple of years, they will be laughing at you."

The ridicule took its toll on Cuneo and Bodine, who were not immune to doubts. One weekend they had gone up to Lake Placid to study up on more sled designs, and they were sharing a room at the training center. There was a knock on the door of Cuneo and Bodine's room. It was Shimer. "Look, I believe you guys have something," Shimer told them. "I know this is going to be a struggle for all of us, but all of us are with you."

One unlikely believer in the Bo-Dyn Project was Michael Nietch, the head bobsled designer for the Germans, who was still in a leadership role with FES as of late 2016.

Throughout the mid-to-early 1990s, Cuneo and Nietch would talk design, bobsleds, how to generate speed, and the differences between the U.S. and German libations. In 1994, when Canadian Bob Storey replaced a German as the head of the ISBF, Cuneo was put on the Bobsled Rules Committee, where he and Nietch became good friends with their shared interests in design. "That was a revolution in 1994," says Kurtz. "When Bob Storey came along, much of the international bobsled architecture started to change. People like Cuneo could be on the Rules Committee, and the rules were written in English in clear and precise language, as opposed to being translated straight from the German. That made our understanding of the rules much better, which helped Bob with the design. It sounds like a small thing, but it was a big deal." When Cuneo and his team would inevitably come up with their latest innovation, Nietch would take Cuneo aside, and say something along the lines of, "I know you did this for a reason, and you are way too smart to have done it incorrectly. But I don't see it."

Because the team knew there was some jealousy surrounding their sleds, the U.S. was ever vigilant during the World Cup races in Europe. Briglia, as the full-time mechanic, would often be around at odd times of the day and night, getting the sleds ready. Briglia was always on the watch for gamesmanship by the sport's icemeisters, which is an actual job. The icemeister is the individual in charge of the track. He grooms the ice; so it's uniformly about an inch thick and between 23 to 25 degrees Fahrenheit, no matter what kind of abuse the ice is taking. The idea is that the ice conditions shouldn't change at all from those encountered during the training runs or from one heat to another, ensuring fairness. Inconsistencies caused by humidity, warming, or rain cannot only lead to a bad performance by a sled, but can be dangerous as well. "Let's put it this way," Briglia says. "You could screw pilots up if you wanted to, and I'd seen some crazy things at some of these tracks. I was very careful to watch the icemeisters that they didn't change the track between races or after training. If we adjusted a certain way and the race day comes, and the ice is very different, then that hurts us, you know what I'm saying?" In fact, it was common knowledge back in the 1980s, and 1990s that track temperatures would often change drastically from one heat to another, making both athletes and coaches wonder what exactly was going on in the refrigeration plants at the various tracks.

Despite his pitbull approach to the icemeisters, Briglia's reputation as one of the masterminds behind the new crop of U.S. sleds drew athletes from other countries to him with questions about the Bo-Dyn sled aerodynamics, about the runners, about the fiberglass. He started getting requests from other countries to look at their sleds and lend parts out.

Soon, weekly poker games started among the circuit's athletes and coaches. Briglia was having a positive influence on the whole vibe of the European bobsled circuit. Sometimes one person's personality can make a huge impact, and Briglia's blend of humor and a little touch of raunchiness was the right one for the time. The circuit, despite — or perhaps because of — the forced togetherness of spending six weeks in Europe in the same small mountain towns, the same restaurants, and the same small hotels, was not an overly friendly place. Briglia helped change that.

"Everyone started getting along," Briglia says. "It became a situation where you didn't hate the athletes from other countries now. There was this new way of doing things; we would have other teams come to us, and we fixed their sleds, so they could race." "Over time, I think Frank softened up the whole bobsled world," says Nancy Pierpoint, who at one point served on both Boards of the Bo-Dyn Project and the USFBF. "Coaches and technicians from other countries would want to go out to dinner with Frank and our team, and that never used to happen."

Between Briglia's duties to the U.S. sliders and his extracurricular efforts circuit-wide, he was working 24/7. Part of the reason for his presence around the sleds, day and night, was that he didn't care to do much else. Briglia ended up living and working in Europe for more than 15 years, but he wasn't a guy who spent a lot of time in cafes and old cathedrals, even if he had had the time. "Europe is great if you like old stuff," Briglia says. "People say all the time, 'Wow, living in Europe all that time, that must have been so great;' but my job wasn't to go to old churches." No, his job, along with Bodine, Cuneo, and the rest of the Bo-Dyn team, was to introduce a NASCAR approach to bobsledding. That they had done, and now it was time to win. But to win, the project would need more help, both financially and organizationally. It needed some new blood.

116

Chapter Five

New Blood, New Faces

IN 1995, CUNEO and Vaillancourt realized that the 2-man and the 4-man sleds were totally different animals. The 2-man sled reacted completely different than the 4-man sled. The extra foot and half of length in the 4-man – about 13 feet long compared to 11.5 feet for the 2-man – just totally changed the aerodynamics. Not to mention the fact that four men over six feet tall, averaging about 230 pounds, had to load into this container as quickly as possible.

Tragically, however, the Bo-Dyn team would have to perfect the 4-man sled without Bobby Vaillancourt. Vaillancourt died of a sudden, massive heart attack in 1996, devastating his friends and colleagues at Chassis Dynamics.

As time went on and most members of Team USA fully bought into Bo-Dyn sleds, Cuneo had more and more data at his disposal. The wind-testing, experimentation, and never-ending search for more speed continued even as drivers and push athletes came and went from the national bobsled team. Shimer had an excellent 1996-1997 campaign, taking home with Randy Jones the first-ever Bo-Dyn bobsled victory with a win in the 2-man World Cup race in Innsbruck in December 1996; and then following up the next weekend for another win in Cortina, again with Jones. Shimer then went on to win bronze medals at the World Championships in St. Moritz in both the 2- and 4-man, becoming the first American since 1950 to medal in both events. The U.S. athletes and their now excellent start times were finally benefiting from world-class sleds. "All of a sudden the U.S. was good," says Morgan, who watched the U.S. progress first-hand as he worked the bobsled circuit with his broadcasting production team. By the time the Nagano Games came in 1998, the U.S. was expected to be in the medal hunt.

Besides constantly trying to think about how to improve the Bo-Dyn sleds, Cuneo had taken on another challenge: ensuring that all teams adhered to the rules. With a few years of bobsled experience under his belt, as well as a lifetime of watching race car teams pushing the envelope regarding the rules, Cuneo was convinced that the pre-race haphazard sled inspection process allowed for – as they say in racing – a "loose" interpretation of the rules. Cuneo knew that Bo-Dyn sleds were not only fast but stuck to what was allowed within the rules of the sport, even while competitors from other countries clearly were getting away with non-compliant sleds. As mentioned earlier, Cuneo, with the help of David Kurtz, successfully lobbied for appointment as the USA representative to the FIBT technical committee and, within four years, was so respected that he was made the head of the committee. Cuneo's fair enforcement of the rules, while not the main reason for the Bo-Dyn sleds' increasing success, was certainly a factor as the sleds started to win.

If not for a mistake in the final run of the 4-man in Nagano, that success would have continued in the Olympic Games. After each of the first two runs (the second heat of the first day was canceled due to thunder and lighting, so the race was comprised of three heats), Shimer's sled was ranked third, in perfect striking distance for a medal. At the bottom part of the track of the third and final run, Shimer and his team were having a great trip down the ice, surging into 2nd place and looking for all the world like the first U.S. bobsled medalists since 1956 at the Cortina Olympics – and silver medalists to boot. Briglia, watching in person at the track, was on the phone with Nancy Pierpoint back in Connecticut giving her a live turn-by-turn color commentary.

All of a sudden, Pierpoint's line went dead. Briglia had inexplicably hung up. An abrupt movement by one of Shimer's push athletes had caused a slight change in the aerodynamics, costing Shimer's sled a few hundredths of a second. The team finished in 5th-place — off the medal stand by two-hundredths of a second — which meant there would be no tsunami of publicity about ending the U.S. bobsled medal drought, no additional sponsors, and no new influx of funds. Sponsors get on board going into Olympics years when medals are a possibility. They jump *off* the bandwagon when the party is over and a team – once again – fails to take home any medals.

If there was one silver lining to come out of Nagano, it was that Briglia and Cuneo experienced an epiphany about the crew dynamics of the 4-man sled. Simply put, the crew was riding too high. "The effect was like a sail in the wind, and it was hurting the aerodynamics," Briglia says. The simplest solution – smaller people – isn't a good option for this particular bobsledding issue, because physics demands some heavy people in the sled, and heavy people are often tall, as well. In later models of the 4-man sled, Cuneo slightly expanded the seating compartment, so the brakeman could get in easily and tuck down into the sled.

Post-Nagano, the momentum started to wane regarding financial support, as the next Games were four years away; and the U.S. team – even with the Bo-Dyn sleds – hadn't yet hit Olympic pay dirt.

So, the fundraising net was cast far and wide. Earle Ashton, a broker at Merrill Lynch who dealt with high net-worth individuals and Phil Hausmann and his wife, Nancy, started hosting fishing tournaments in Pompano Beach, Florida, to raise money for the sleds, which were at this point costing about $30,000 to $75,000 each. One of Shimer's sleds even read "Spirit of Florida."

And NASCAR? Continually bringing the NASCAR sponsorship and promotional magic to bobsledding wasn't easy. Take an iconic sports sponsor like Budweiser, for example. Bud's marketers love that a race car with the Bud logo is going to go around and around for a certain number of laps before tens of thousands of fans and a national television audience. With bobsleds, U.S. network TV coverage happens once every four years at the Olympics, and at the Olympics, sleds can't even advertise corporate logos (In Europe, conversely, TV ratings are high for bobsledding in Germany and Switzerland, among other nations).

But Bo-Dyn's friends and partners, many with their own connections to racing, were determined to try. Since Connecticut had such a connection to regional and national auto racing, Cuneo family friend, Pierpoint, got involved. Her late husband had been a drag racer and had worked with Cuneo over the years, as had Pierpoint herself in various roles. Pierpoint helped plan a series of road shows throughout Connecticut and New York with some of the new Bo-Dyn sleds accompanied by various bobsled pilots and NASCAR drivers. Bodine and his brothers, Todd and Brett, Randy LaJoie, and Kyle Petty were frequent headliners.

The race fans loved it, of course. There were silent auctions and dinners with racers; at $100 a ticket, these nights were a lot of fun for NASCAR fans. For a chance to sit next to Bodine, or Petty, or LaJoie, they had no problem coming out to support the bobsled cause. One fundraiser featured an auctioning off of the White Tornado, the old beloved modified race car of Bodine's, which was found and restored by Cuneo. A financial heavy-hitter bid on and won the car – which he then gave to Bodine at the end of the night. Another event auctioned off the quarter-panel from a car that Bodine had hit in a short track race after he suffered a cheap shot from that car's driver. The room erupted in laughter when the quarter-panel was put up for sale and erupted again in applause when the relic was sold for $1,500.

Meanwhile, the USBSF Board was still flummoxed about what to think of all of these NASCAR-affiliated fund-raisers. "You know, I think the Board in those days thought we were a bunch of redneck yahoos," Pierpoint says. "But we didn't care; the vast majority of Board members at that point were doing it to enhance their obituaries."

But there was another way to get funding. For some time, Cuneo had been going to the USBSF with grant proposals to win funding from the USOC's Sports Science Foundation. Cuneo would come up with a specific idea to research – say it had to do with wind-testing – and then would work through the USBSF to apply for funding to the USOC. Cuneo helped the USBSF win a number of these grants. In fact, Cuneo was so successful at formulating winning grant proposals that at a USOC Sports Science Foundation summit, he was invited to give a presentation to representatives of other Olympic sports – both summer and winter – on how to put together a professional grant application.

That's what was going on off the track. On the track, Shimer, 36 years old after Nagano, had a pilot named Todd Hays nipping at his heels. Hays, a fantastic athlete who had been a linebacker on the Tulsa University football team, as well as the 1993 national kickboxing champion, would soon become the new face of American bobsledding. His talent was matched by a fierce competitiveness that often rubbed teammates the wrong way. This was a man, after all, who was just as at home yelling at his push athletes for supposed indiscretions as he was blaming Bo-Dyn sleds for losses in post-race television interviews. Hays, never a believer in the Bo-Dyn Project, would go on to cause friction between the USBSF and Bo-Dyn for the rest of his career.

But the 1998-1999 season also saw a new face on Team USA — a quiet, introverted man who appeared the polar opposite of Hays in every way. Steve Holcomb was a former junior ski champ from Park City, Utah. Holcomb was an excellent athlete in the mode of a Brian Shimer, fast and powerful. But Holcomb also had a sixth sense borne of the natural athlete who had been exposed to just about any sport one can think of. "I literally was outside almost every day of my life playing some kind of sport," Holcomb says. You name it, Holcomb had done it. Ball sports – Little League All-Star shortstop, check; high school football player, check; competitive soccer player, check – the fine motor sports (archery, golf); and outdoor sports such as skiing, rock climbing, and mountain biking – yup, he did those too.

In fact, bobsled was the one sport he had *not* done by the time he graduated from the Winter Sports School, even though one of the only world-class sliding tracks in the country was right next door to his school. Holcomb had wanted to go to the Olympics as a skier so had never really thought twice about the track. The problem was, and it was hard for Holcomb to admit this to himself as a teenager, he just wasn't fast enough to be an Olympic skier.

At 18 years of age and sensing that his career in skiing might come to an end with the U.S. West Regional Junior National Team, Holcomb decided on a whim to attend an organizational meeting for the Alpine Bobsled Club at the Wasatch Brew Pub in Park City. The problem? At that very time, there was also a tryout for the local Park City Muckers Rugby Sevens. "You know, I was leaning toward rugby because I thought it was a really cool sport," Holcomb says. "Then again, I probably wouldn't have been an Olympian in rugby." Luckily for U.S. bobsledding, Holcomb chose the Alpine Bobsled Club meeting.

Holcomb walked into the pub and sat down, only to have a bouncer approach him almost immediately, asking for his ID. "I mean, within 30 seconds they kicked me out of the bar," Holcomb says. On the way out, he told the bouncer why he was there, and the bouncer told him to leave his contact information. A few weeks later, he was invited to a tryout, where he scored 675 points in a six-event test consisting of three sprints, a shot put test, and two agility drills. In turned out that 675 was the minimum score to make the U.S. men's "B" team.

Holcomb was thrilled but, also, a little shocked at how his bobsled career, after one day, had already eclipsed his skiing career that he had worked on so hard for years. "I was like, 'Wow, I just went from struggling to make the "D" team in skiing to being on the "B" team after my first day,'" Holcomb says. A few months later, he found himself in Lake Placid at the National Push Championships, and his career was off. His reaction to those first days in Lake Placid? "Let's just say I grew up in Park City, which is a pretty small town," Holcomb says. "But it's a metropolis compared to Lake Placid. When I realized that this was the town that hosted the 1980 Olympics, my first thought was, 'How did anyone find this place?'"

Holcomb made his debut in November 1998 as the brakeman on Shimer's 2-man sled, finishing 17th in a World Cup race in Calgary. Holcomb would gain experience over the next three years as a brakeman for Shimer, Hays, and Mike Dionne. When Holcomb was diagnosed in 2002 with Keratoconus, a degenerative eye disease that affects 1 in 1,000 people, he didn't tell anyone, including teammates Shimer and Hays. He decided he needed to fight through it on his own and manage the condition as best he could, as an eye transplant – the only known cure — would put his career on hold for years. It was a decision that a few years later, would not only nearly cost him his career, but also his sight.

But for U.S. bobsledding, the years between 1998 and 2002 were really about Shimer and Hays, the two American mainstays during this period. Jim Herberich was also still piloting at a high level, but the good and bad angels of Team USA were the ones setting the tone, Shimer with his sunny disposition and elder statesman status, and Hays with his aggressive defiance.

Interestingly, in their own ways, their methods worked for both of them. "It's true that Todd had a difficult personality," says Shimer. "Everyone knew that. But in an odd way, he pushed me, and I pushed him. And he pushed the Bo-Dyn folks by never being satisfied." During the years between the Nagano and the Salt Lake City Games, Shimer's best results at the World Championships – the biggest event for bobsledders other than the Olympics — in the 2-man was a 5th-place finish in 1999 with brakeman Pavle Jovanovic in Cortina d'Ampezzo in Italy. In 2001, the year before the Olympic Games, Hays and his brakeman, Garrett Hines, had a very good season but finished off the podium.

But it was really in the 4-man where the Bo-Dyn continuing improvements shown through. Team Shimer – with various push athletes, including Dave Owens, Mike Kohn, Garrett Hines, Doug Sharp, and Dan Steele – finished in the top five in three out of the four World Championships. "At that point, I think Cuneo had figured out the aerodynamics, how the sled should accommodate the four athletes, had perfected the steering mechanism, all that," Latour says. "At that point, it was really on the right day, with the right athletes, on the right track."

But the effort still needed money. Coming out of Nagano, the kitty was empty, and the shelves were bare. Geoff Bodine had run out of money, was facing divorce as well as the bankruptcy of his race car team, and the federation didn't have any money given the dearth of medals from the Olympics. Cuneo and his team in Oxford, Connecticut were essentially working for free. "I put everything I owned in jeopardy," Cuneo says. Even some of the charity events, like a 2001 fishing tournament, the money would go to the federation as a matter of protocol, but then the money would be spent on other bills and never make it back to Cuneo. "Bob's guys were not getting paid," says John Morgan.

As the Salt Lake City Games approached, it was time for a reckoning. Team USA had two world-class 4-man teams. The Americans and the Germans, in fact, were pushing each other, as Cuneo and Nitsch were competing for bragging rights. As for the women, this would be the first Olympics ever for women's bobsled, and during the pre-Olympic season, American Jean Racine had won six of eight races and was one of the favorites for the gold in Park City. Her teammate, Jill Bakken, was also expected to do well; and both were driving Bo-Dyn sleds.

Then there was Bodine, of course, the man who started it all. Bodine, 52 years old and ten years removed from his decision to build American sleds for American athletes, was planning to attend the Salt Lake Games along with his son, Barry. He arrived in Salt Lake about a week into the Games, getting up early to watch and mix with the Team USA sliders as they prepared. Just a few days before, he'd had a great Daytona 500 with a Top 10 finish. But this is what had him excited. The women's team would also be making their first ever Olympic competition too, and all of them would be using Bo-Dyn sleds.

Everyone affiliated with Bo-Dyn was hungry for medals. But then again, they had been confident in Nagano, as well. This would be the third Olympic Games for Bo-Dyn sleds. If Team USA were shut out again, no amount of Cuneo engineering magic would be able to fix it.

Chapter Six

The Night Train Team Starts to Take Shape

BRIAN SHIMER POINTED toward the Utah mountains in the distance. "When the sun goes behind those mountains," he said to a friend, "the track is really fast, from about 4:17 p.m. to 4:26 p.m. If I can draw between 15th and 20th in the 4-man, we could really nail it."

The heady days before an Olympic event are a time of optimism, hope, and confidence. With the first heat of the 2002 Olympic bobsledding competition still 48 hours away, no mistakes had been made; no potential had gone unfulfilled. Every bobsled pilot could see the perfect line; every team could imagine gold.

The 2002 games were the second consecutive Winter Games in which every bobsled driven by United States athletes had been a product of the Bo-Dyn Project, and the third Games in which Bo-Dyn bobsleds were used. Going into the Salt Lake City Games, it was the always controversial Todd Hays who was the top American bobsled pilot. Father Time and injuries had robbed Shimer of the start-time sprinting speed that many had noticed more than a decade earlier.

In fact, a couple of months before the Games, Shimer had been left behind in the early part of the season, not accompanying the team to Europe. Even during Olympic trials training in Salt Lake City earlier that winter, he had to talk third-tier push athletes into jumping into the sled with him to train. Still, Shimer felt all along that he could compete on the Salt Lake City track, and he indeed qualified for the Games at the U.S. Olympic Trials. His driving experience was still second to none in the world, and if he could get the start draw number he wanted —somewhere between 15-20 — Shimer knew he would be able to shock the legion of non-believers.

But it's important to remember that it wasn't just the men who were trying to ride Bo-Dyn sleds into history at the Salt Lake City Games. Before the men's competition, there was the first-ever women's bobsled competition, as women's bobsled had been voted in as a sport in the autumn of 1999. Jill Bakken and Vonetta Flowers won the gold medal in the inaugural competition by 3/10 of a second over a pair from Germany. Forget about bobsledding — Flowers was the first African-American woman to win a medal in any sport in the Winter Olympics, period! Bakken, like Shimer on the men's side, had been having a forgettable World Cup season and wasn't even invited to the European leg of the women's World Cup circuit. So, her appearance atop the podium also made for a great story.

The women were also mired in controversy, as both Bakken and Jean Racine, the top American drivers, dropped their long-time push athletes shortly before the Olympic trials, opting to choose another brakewoman. While it worked out for Bakken with Flowers, Racine finished fifth with pusher Gea Johnson, who unfortunately was hampered at the Olympics with a hamstring injury. Bottom line: it was the first Olympic bobsled medal for the USA Bobsled Team since 1956, and it was the first Olympic medal for the Bo-Dyn Project — but it would not be the last at these games.

In the 2-man competition, Shimer finished 9th with brakeman Darrin Steele. Hays and brakeman Garrett Hines finished 4th, just three-hundredths out of America's first 2-man bobsled medal since 1952. Germany's Cristoph Langen took home the gold.

As it turned out, Shimer drew the 17th slot for the 4-man, perfect for his pre-race plans to fly down the track at the most sled-friendly time of the day. The version of Shimer who showed up at the mountain on race day for the first two heats was the intense, focused athlete who had gone missing the past year or two. "What I always respected about Brian," says Cuneo, "is that on race day he had a game face like no one else. He had started to lose that a little bit after his prime years; the Europeans weren't afraid of him anymore. But that day the 4-man competition started in Salt Lake City, he showed up on the hill with that killer look of his."

After three heats, Shimer's sled was in 4th place. On a track that emphasized start time, as it was relatively short, Shimer was well outside of the top 10 in start times. But he was making up time the old-fashioned way, with his driving skills. Between the third and fourth heats, Shimer also displayed the leadership that would one day propel him to the head coaching position of the U.S. squad. Hays was acting distracted and highly agitated, even though he was in 3rd place going into the fourth and final run. The pressure of trying to break a U.S. men's medal drought that stretched back to 1956, in front of a raucous U.S. home crowd no less, was gnawing at him. It was Shimer who helped calm Hays down and refocus him. When Hays acknowledged Shimer's help afterward, it was the only time anyone could remember Hays ever humbly expressing such a sentiment.

In his final run, Shimer and his team dramatically pulled into 1st place with the top three sleds still to come, including Hays, who held a huge .24 second lead. Swiss and German teams would follow Hays to close out the competition. With at least one American foursome guaranteed a medal – and the distinct possibility of a second spot on the podium depending on how the Swiss and Germans finished — the U.S. men's 46-year bobsledding medal drought was guaranteed to come to an end. When Hays crossed the finish line in his fourth and final heat, his sled had *just* edged Shimer by .05 of a second, even though he had beaten Shimer in cumulative starting times by .35 of a second over the four trips down the mountain. When the Swiss team then came in with a time that dropped them behind Shimer, the hometown crowd exploded in a celebration that sounded more like the inside of a college football stadium than the bottom of a bobsled track. "It was wonderful to hear," says Geoff Bodine. "After that Swiss team finished, I was having a flashback to 10 years earlier, watching those Olympics in Albertville." Germany's Andre Lange was the last sled down, and Lange took home the first gold medal of his stellar career.

Hays had come out on top in the medal hunt, but Shimer – along with his teammates Mike Kohn, Doug Sharp, and Dan Steele — had clinched a medal first. "It was appropriate that Shimer broke the U.S. medal drought," Morgan says. "No one has ever had a better four heats driving a bobsled than Shimer in Salt Lake." Wolfgang Hoppe, the German bobsled pilot who is still the most decorated Olympic driver in history with six medals, told anyone who would listen after the race that Shimer's bronze medal represented some of the best bobsled driving he'd ever seen.

At the 2002 Winter Olympic Games, then, Bo-Dyn Project sleds had already helped create a significant bit of history, as the U.S. men and women won three bobsled competition medals (one gold, one silver, and one bronze).

Four years earlier, after the U.S. had been shut out at the Nagano Olympic bobsled competition, money was scarce. But after the 2002 Games, the USBSF received significant support from the USOC. For Chassis Dynamics, the 2002

Olympic results and the subsequent cash infusion came just in the nick of time. Cuneo and his fabricators, mechanics, and technicians hadn't been paid in months. In fact, they had done an enormous amount of work for which that they would never get paid. At least after Salt Lake City, they could count on getting compensated for their labor. "Nobody on our team got paid for quite a while; we just did the work," Cuneo says. "From about 2000 on, there wasn't a lot of money coming in. After Salt Lake City, things got a lot better."

It isn't just the official spigot of money that gets turned on after a successful Olympic Games. Dan Goodwin, for example, a Virginia-based attorney who served for several years on the USBSF Board and eventually became one of the core members of the Bo-Dyn Project Board from 2006 on, tells the story of how, in the summer after the 2002 Games, his fundraising efforts on behalf of Olympian Mike Kohn suddenly became a lot more successful. Kohn was a push athlete on Shimer's bronze medal sled, and the annual golf tournament that Goodwin spear-headed on behalf of Kohn usually brought in a very healthy $6,000 or $7,000. Things changed after Kohn's silver medal. "The tournament in 2002 after the Olympics was our biggest year; of course, it was just wild," Goodwin says. "We had the berets that the team had worn at the Games, some Olympic jackets, and just a whole bunch of stuff to auction. We held the golf tournament, a dinner, and then a great auction. It helped keep this thing going for Mike Kohn for another couple of years."

Soon an avenue for funding appeared. Not far away from Chassis Dynamics in Oxford, Connecticut was the headquarters of a company that would soon become synonymous with the Bo-Dyn Project.

*****

The Chester, Connecticut headquarters of Whelen Engineering stands a couple of hours' drive from New York City, in the south-central part of the state. The first thing to know about Whelen is that the company in 2016 epitomizes everything Bodine believed nearly a quarter of a century ago about the benefits of American manufacturing and innovation.

Whelen designs and manufactures safety lights for emergency and other non-conventional vehicles, from fire trucks to police cruisers; from snow plows to tow trucks; from jets skis to all-terrain vehicles. It also makes aviation-related lighting as well as what's called "mass notification" systems, designed for warning the public in the event of disasters like tsunamis, floods, or tornadoes. The company was founded in

1948- USA Bobsled Team that won the Olympic 4-man gold medal in St. Moritz. It would be the last Olympic gold medal for USA Men's Bobsled until 2010.

Hazel Franklin, pictured with the legendary Lyon Mountain Bobsled Team and driving the historic "Ironshoes Bobsled" built in 1933 by Bob Linney. Pictured here is his son, Bill Linney, with John Kerr, Jerry Blanch, and Angus Clain. "Ironshoes"was the first all-metal bobsled and the first with cast-iron runners instead of steel runners.

The awards ceremony for the 1932 Olympic Games 4-man bobsled in Lake Placid, NY. The event was held the day after the Closing Ceremonies, with Team USA members Billy Fiske, Eddie Egan, Clifford Gray, and Jay O'Brien taking home the gold medal.

Billy Fiske, at the 1932 Winter Olympic Games in Lake Placid, NY, receiving the Martineau Cup which has been awarded to the 4-man bobsled World Champions since 1930.

General Motors bobsled in 1965. The bobsled was sleek, but when the U.S. argued about who was going to pilot the sled, General Motors disappeared.

Excalibur Sled 1980 Lake Placid. (L-R) James "Nitro" Morgan, Red Hogle, and David Stevens the Excalibur Designer.

Left: ArtTyler, an engineer and physicist from Kodak, built the most successful 4-man bobsled of its time, winning an Olympic bronze medal in 1956 and the World Championship in 1959. His innovations of a tear-drop cowling and independent suspension were ahead of his time. Cuneo and Vaillancourt spend lots of time looking at this bobsled. It was not until 2002 that the USA Bobsled Team won Olympic medals again and then the Night Train won the World Championship in 2009 (the first in 50 years) and Olympic gold in 2010 (the first in 62 years).

The "Tyler sled" was the last United States bobsled to win a World Championship in 1959 and the last Olympic medal since 1956. (L-R) Bob Vaillancourt and Bob Cuneo at Lake Placid, NY in 1993.

Bo-Dyn debut at Lake Placid in January 1993 after the Roselli run. Team Provolone and athletes together at the USOTC. Back row (L-R) James Purvis, Bob Cuneo, Garret Hines, Don Barker, Mike Briglia, and Dave Butkevich. Kneeling behind bobsled Bruce Russell. In sled- Geoff Bodine, Bob Vaillancourt. In front of the bobsled- Brian Shimer, Frank Briglia.

Right: First Bo-Dyn prototype bobsled, 1993. (L-R) Bob Cuneo, Bob Vaillancourt.

Hilti 2-man bobsled rebuilt for Shimer in 1993.

Our cabin in Lillehammer at the 1994 Winter Olympic Games- Back row (L-R) Don Barker, Simon (of Featherlite Germany), Mike Curiel (of SAS Airlines), Holly (of SAS Airlines), Frank Briglia, Ludwig Meuller (of Featherlite Germany). Front row (L-R) Bob Vaillancourt, Melissa Fogel (of SAS Airlines), Angelo Guerrera, Ken Armstrong (of PI Research/IBM).

Team Provolone ready for Nagano in 1997- (L-R) Frank Briglia, Angelo Guerrera, Tom Centenaro, and Bob Cuneo.

Bob Cuneo and Bob Vaillancourt in 1995, just before Bob Vaillancourt's death.

Salt Lake Winter Olympics in 2002- the USA Bobsled 4-man team won bronze, first USA Men's medal since 1956. (L-R) Dan Steele, Brian Shimer, Mike Kohn, and Doug Sharp.

Brian Shimer and Randy Jones at Winterberg in 1996, the year the Bo-Dyn bobsled started winning.

Brian Shimer drove flawlessly on his way to the Olympic bronze medal.

NASCAR® drivers for the Inaugural Geoff Bodine Bobsled Challenge-2006 in Lake Placid, NY.

Drivers for the 2007 Geoff Bodine Bobsled Challenge.

Drivers for the 2008 Geoff Bodine Bobsled Challenge.

Drivers for the 2009 Geoff Bodine Bobsled Challenge in front of the new Whelen/BO-Dyn Bobsled Garage.

Drivers for the 2010 Geoff Bodine Bobsled Challenge.

2007-08 USA Bobsled and Skeleton Team outfitted with their Columbia clothing, provided by the Bo-Dyn Bobsled Project.

2009- Team Holcomb and
The Night Train, winning the first
World Championship in 4-man
bobsled for the USA in 50 years!

Vonetta Flowers and Jill Bakken
winning the Women's Gold medal at
the 2002 Winter Olympic Games in
Salt Lake. It was the first women's
bobsled Olympic competition, and
Flowers was the first African American
athlete to win a Winter Olympic
Games gold medal.

Erin Pac and Elana Meyers
winning the Olympic bronze
medal at the 2010 Winter
Olympics in a radically
designed Bo-Dyn chassis
that Bob Cuneo talked Erin
into trying two weeks
before the games!

Erin Pac and Elana Meyers receiving their
Olympic bronze medal at the 2010 Winter
Olympic Games in Vancouver, B.C., Canada.

Andre Lange, winner of the previous four Olympic gold medals (gold in 4-man in 2002, gold in 2-man and 4-man in 2006, and gold in 2-man in 2010) congratulating Steve Holcomb at the flower ceremony immediately after the 2010 gold medal performance in Vancouver, B.C., Canada.

Team Holcomb holding Gold, Vancouver 2010

Team Holcomb and The Night Train in the final turn of the gold medal run at the 2010 Winter Olympic Games in Vancouver, B.C., Canada.

Team with Geoff 5 minutes after 2010 Gold medal.

Team Holcomb on the podium at the 2010 Winter Olympic Games in Vancouver, B.C., Canada.

Bo-Dyn Bobsled Project Board of Directors- (L-R) John Morgan (Executive Director), Phil Kurze (President), Geoff Bodine (Founder/Vice President), John Vester (CFO), and Dan Goodwin (Secretary/Legal Counsel).

No one bonded more closely with the Bo-Dyn Bobsled Project than Brian Shimer (pictured with Geoff Bodine). In the early years, when many were doubting the Project, Shimer stood front and center to offer "Team Provolone" everything needed.

Steve Holcomb will never be forgotten, not only for his accomplishments in the sport of bobsledding but most importantly, for probably being the most liked bobsled athlete that ever lived.

1952 by George Washington Whelen, III who designed an anti-collision beacon in the garage behind his house.

As Phil Kurze, Whelen's Vice President of Motorsports as well as Vice President of the company's Mass Notification business, leads a visitor through the hallways of the 240,000 square foot headquarters – stuffed with memorabilia not only from Whelen's corporate successes but also the triumphs associated with its racing sponsorships – he points out a framed original product sheet for George Whelen's original beacon. "Actually this was designed for aviation, and we still have an aviation division today," he says. "But early on, George Whelen realized that it could be mounted on police motorcycles and police cars, fire trucks, ambulances, basically any kind of public service vehicle," Kurze says. "And that's what put Whelen Engineering on the map."

Walking the halls of Whelen, past the machine shops, past the testing labs, past the packaging area where the company makes its own bubble wrap, it's abundantly clear that this is not a standard-issue corporate headquarters: things are *made* here. In fact, Whelen is the only U.S. maker of emergency warning equipment that manufactures virtually all of its products entirely in the United States. How does it compete this way? The use of advanced technologies like robotics, yes; a motivated and talented workforce of 1,100, certainly; but as Kurze tells it, it's also the overall commitment to "Made in America."

Whelen's competitors import many of their component parts from overseas, but such a practice is anathema to Whelen. "About ninety percent of our products are made in America," says Kurze "We mold all of our lenses, all of our plastic parts. We have a metal shop where we cut and drill and stamp all of the metal parts we need." In other words, Whelen even makes some of its own nuts, bolts, and screws. Written on the side of the company's 18-wheeler truck that shuttles daily between the Chester facility and a bigger manufacturing plant in Charleston, New Hampshire, are the words: "American employees, American manufacturing, American pride." Kurze is asked what it would take for other U.S. companies to recommit to manufacturing in their home country in the same manner that Whelen has. "It can be done," he says. "Whelen competes through technology and hiring great talent. That means other companies can do it as well."

Whelen's former company President and CEO is John Olson, who in early 2016 stepped back from day-to-day operations of the company after 38 years. "American innovation is second to none, and that's how we always approached expanding our business," Olson explains. It was Olson, a graduate of the University of New Hampshire, and Kurze, an alum of nearby Central Connecticut State University who realized that talented engineers did not have to come from India, Japan, or even the Ivy League – they were right in their Northeast backyard, at UNH and Central Connecticut's excellent engineering schools.

Whelen even has a program where students from Central Connecticut, after finishing their junior year, spend the next 12 months as full-time salaried employees of the company, earn some additional scholarship money for their senior year, and – if all goes well – land a job at Whelen after graduation. "We've hired several great engineers through that program," Kurze says.

But does Whelen pay the price in any way for the deliberately local feel to its employees? On the contrary — Whelen's penchant for home-grown engineering talent, together with the best technology available, have made it the industry leader with a reputation for manufacturing innovation.

When it's suggested to Kurze that Whelen could be more profitable if it moved some manufacturing overseas,

Kurze reacts like he just saw a 90-watt bulb lighting the wing of a 747 jet. "We can make superior equipment in America," Kurze says. "We have the talent; we have risk-takers; we have the best universities!"

Why is Whelen Engineering so important to a story about building American-made bobsleds? Because firms like Whelen fly in the face of the common mantra today concerning American manufacturing: it can't be revived because of the expense, relative dearth of trained engineers, and onerous regulations. Whelen proves it *can* be done in America, whether it's police car lights or, as Bob Cuneo's Chassis Dynamics also proved, bobsleds.

******

Kurze had come to Whelen in 1993 for a sales and marketing job, just when the Bo-Dyn Project was gaining speed. Ever since he went to his first car race at the age of five in 1954, Kurze was fascinated with auto racing. When one of the engineers at Whelen said that his father had a race team that was active in a local touring series, Kurze pounced.

A man named Ted Marsh was the owner of the race team, and Kurze asked what it would cost for Whelen to be on the car. The result? A 5" x 2" decal on the side of the car. After a little research, Kurze determined that Whelen's customers for its warning lights and sirens – police, fire, ambulances, and utilities – were huge racing fans. He doubled down, and that initial decal eventually morphed into primary sponsorship of the car in the NASCAR Busch Series, the second tier of three national series (known today as the Xfinity Series). By the mid-1990s, Whelen had a high profile driver named Steve Park at the wheel of the car, and Whelen's motor sports program was going along great guns, even getting television exposure through the Busch Series.

About that time, Kurze heard that Geoff Bodine, the Yankee driver that had gone down south to become a NASCAR driver, was not happy with the sponsor of his NASCAR Winston Cup car, QVC. After a race at the famed Watkins Glen race track in upstate New York in 1996, Kurze saw Bodine by his car. Luckily, Kurze had a conversation starter. He had read an interview with Bodine after that year's Daytona 500 that mentioned the Bo-Dyn Project. As luck would have it, Kurze' old fraternity brother from Central Connecticut State was none other than John Morgan, the Olympic bobsledding broadcaster. Morgan and Kurze had not seen each other since 1973.

So Kurze introduced himself, telling Geoff that they had a mutual friend in the bobsled world. After a minute of small talk about the Bo-Dyn Project, Kurze asked point blank what it would cost for Whelen to become an associate sponsor on Bodine's race car. Bodine thanked Kurze for his interest and said he had to talk to his business people and that he'd call Kurze the next day. Two colleagues of Kurze' who were with him that weekend had a good chuckle after they left the pit crew area. "They were pretty much laughing at me," Kurze says. "Saying, 'Sure, Geoff Bodine is going to call you tomorrow.'"

The next day the phone rang, and it was none other than Bodine on the line, along with a business colleague. The deal was hammered out, and the boy who had always loved racing had bagged one of the biggest drivers on the scene. The Whelen logo was on Bodine's race car for that season.

As Kurze got to know Bodine, he saw the sacrifices that the NASCAR star was making for the Bo-Dyn Project. Kurze attended the fishing tournaments in Florida in 2000 and 2001; he saw Bodine and his friends auction off race car parts and memorabilia. All of this effort, time, and resources were being spent to honor Bodine's idea that the country that put a man on the moon had enough superior technology and collective willpower to design the best bobsled in the world. Kurze became more and more interested in Bodine's quest. "I bought into what Geoff was doing big-time," Kurze said. "I wanted to get involved, and I wanted to get Whelen involved."

Kurze explained to Whelen's leadership team what the Bo-Dyn Project would mean for the company. A big selling point internally at Whelen was that the "Made in America" parallels. Both Whelen and the Bo-Dyn Project were committed to manufacturing – and beating the competition with – products built in America.

But Morgan, too, did his part to help win over Whelen executives. In late 2003, he supplied Kurze with demographics and TV ratings proving that European and American audiences for bobsledding were there to be courted. "When people saw our corporate logo on the sleds," Kurze explains, "We wanted them to say, 'Wow, those sleds are high-tech and high-performance vehicles. Those guys must be smart and make really good lights.'"

After the Salt Lake City Games, Whelen started increasing the value of their sponsorship. All in all, through the Vancouver Games in 2010, the company would provide more than $3 million in support of the Bo-Dyn Project.

Like others before, Kurze and Whelen stepped in at a crucial time for the Bo-Dyn Project. At that point, Bodine had put about $400,000 of his own money into the project. Bodine was not only out of funds, but it was also clear that more hands-on leadership was needed to hunt for new sponsorships, bring new ideas, and infuse new blood into the project. In 2003, Cuneo approached Kurze with a surprising offer: In addition to the financial commitment Whelen was going to make, would Kurze personally want to serve as President of the Bo-Dyn Bobsled Project to try to inject some new life into it? Kurze thought about it hard – for about 10 seconds. He took the job.

Back on the track, an afterthought at those Salt Lake City Games was Holcomb, who spent his hometown Games as a forerunner, or one of the drivers who make several runs down the track before each Olympic racing session to ensure the course is okay for competition. In a strange way, the Salt Lake City Olympics represented the perfect transition from Holcomb the push athlete to Holcomb the driver, even though he was devastated that his injury kept him from competing in Shimer's sled. While he had piloted a bobsled for fun 30 or 40 times in the past, Salt Lake City was really Holcomb's driving debut of sorts, even though he wasn't taking part as a competitor. "Especially being at my home track, it really whets my appetite to succeed as a pilot and get back to another Olympics," Holcomb says. It was settled – Holcomb was a driver for good. But no one had any inkling whatsoever just how dominant and decorated Holcomb would eventually become.

In the autumn of 2002, Tuffy Latour took Holcomb and Steve Mesler up to Calgary for about ten days for driver training. Mesler and Holcomb had already forged a terrific relationship, as they had come into the sport just a couple of years apart and had personalities that complemented one another. If Holcomb came into the sport somewhat indirectly from skiing, Mesler had a much more roundabout path.

As a youngster, Mesler had always dreamed of being in the Olympics, and started competing at Junior Olympic track and field meets at age 11. By the time he had graduated high school, Mesler was the national champion in the indoor pentathlon. He was recruited by Duke, Princeton – all of the top schools in the country. But Mesler wanted to attend the college that enabled him to compete at the highest athletic level and eventually achieve his dream: the track and field powerhouse, the University of Florida. "If you wanted to go to the Olympics in track and field, Florida was where you went back then," Mesler says. "I did not want to be a big fish in a little pond. I wanted to be a big fish in the ocean."

147

One hazard of Mesler's chosen sport was overtraining. A competitor in the decathlon has ten sports to work on and could spend an athletic lifetime trying to improve in any one of them, much less all 10. In his freshmen year, competing in the year-ending SEC track and field championships, Mesler suffered an ankle injury. He red-shirted his sophomore year, which decathletes often do anyway to mature a bit and put oneself in the strongest position as a junior and senior. In his third year at Florida and using his second year of eligibility, Mesler blew out his ankle again, this time in the long jump. In his fourth year, it was an elbow injury that sidelined Mesler. He got the message. Even though he planned on going on to graduate school, he passed on his last year of eligibility. "After four years of injury, I really couldn't face another year of that," Mesler recalls.

That autumn of 2000, Mesler was applying to grad schools and various jobs while awaiting his elbow surgery. He then experienced the most important day of his life. "I remember I was two days out of elbow surgery," Mesler says. "I was sitting on my couch, and reflecting and thinking that I didn't want my athletic career to be over. I didn't want to be a has-been at age 22."

But what exactly would he do? Mesler went on the Yahoo! search engine and researched Olympic sports. He thought that bobsledding might potentially be a fit, so he sent a blind email to a USOC email address he found. He described how big he was, how fast he was, and how much weight he could lift. But he also issued a plaintive plea to please; please give him a look. He ended his email with: "Can I do this? If I can, let me know. If I can't, let me know that too, and you'll never hear from me again."

Those were the kinds of emails, in fact, that the U.S. bobsled coaches were all too used to getting forwarded to them from the USOC. Coaches like Shimer and Latour would receive emails over the transom advertising an incredible athletic skillset, only to follow up with a college coach and find out that the athlete overstated his time in the 100-meter dash by three-quarters of a second. "I can't tell you how many times I was in the USA bobsled office over the years, and the coaches would get these ridiculous emails that didn't check out," Mesler says. "As for my email, I think there was an element of 'my life has fallen apart; please throw me a bone here.' I think they took pity on me." (Years later, two days after the Night Train won the gold medal in the 2010 Olympics in Vancouver, a coach named Greg Sand handed

Mesler a print-out of the original email he had written to the USOC).

The very next day after he sent that email, Mesler learned that his Olympic dream wasn't quite dead yet, after all. He received an email back from Sand saying that at 180 pounds he'd need to gain weight, but that if his numbers accurately reflected his talent, he had the potential tools. After a few months of training on his own, Mesler reported in June 2001 to San Diego's Chula Vista Olympic Training Center. The first thing he noticed was that Sand was right — he was going to have to gain weight. "I remember walking into the training center and seeing these ginormous guys. I just couldn't believe how big bobsledders were," Mesler says. But his decathlete skills soon impressed and when selection time came in October, Mesler found out he would be on the team, paired with driver, Mike Dion, in Dion's 2-man sled. Mesler remembered some the veterans he had met in California during training camp who had been cut and only then realized the brutal, Darwinian nature of the push athlete selection process. "The best and worst thing about being a push athlete is that the learning curve is not steep," Mesler says. "If you have the tools and pick up the technique, you can replace someone, even if they are a respected veteran. At the same time, all it takes is someone who's bigger, stronger, and faster than you to show up, and that's it – you're replaced."

Mesler was so ecstatic at being on the U.S. team that he didn't even mind living four to a room at the Olympic Training Center in Lake Placid. "Here I was, after all of those disappointments in track and field, training in Lake Placid to represent the U.S.," Mesler says. "It was ridiculous, at my age living with three other dudes in a tiny room; but to me, it was a blast."

Holcomb welcomed Mesler to the Olympic Training Center and the pair quickly bonded over a similarly quirky sense of humor. "You know, me and Holcomb were also just a bit younger than Todd and Brian and some of the other guys, so we were a little goofier," Mesler says. One such episode became known as the "Holcy" dance mix. Mesler would often get songs stuck in his head and start inserting his friends' names into a song as a joke. Sometime on the road in the winter of 2004, he couldn't get the Digital Underground Hip-Hop tune "Humpty Dance" out of his head, especially the line "The humpty dance is your chance, your chance to do the hump." Mesler got to the track that day, saw Holcomb doing some warm-up exercises, and started to sing, "The Holcy dance is your chance to do the Holcy," upon which Holcomb broke into what was by all accounts some of the worst "white guy" dancing imaginable.

The routine became a hallmark of theirs in their World Cup travels in the years ahead. For example, two years later in Torino, right before Holcomb's first 4-man heat, Mesler yelled out his cue for Holcomb to do the Holcy dance, and his buddy complied in full view of many of his competitors. In fact, Holcomb would do the Holcy dance on command all over the world. There are YouTube videos of Holcomb doing the Holcy dance in European cobblestone alleys, on bobsled tracks, in gyms, in traditional German haufbrau houses, in media interviews, and with teammates, friends, and coaches. In these videos, it's a close call which is worse, Holcomb's dancing or Mesler's singing that accompanies most of the Holcy dance routines.

But well before the Holcy dancing days, when Latour brought Holcomb and Mesler to Calgary for those driving sessions in 2002, he wasn't sure who would emerge as the better driver. Soon enough it was Holcomb who started to display some real driving talent, and it dawned on coaches and teammates that Holcomb's background in ski racing had given him a sixth sense in choosing which line to choose to best get his sled down the hill. "You could start to see that he was going to be pretty special, a pretty talented guy," Latour says. "He definitely opened some eyes, because his decision-making already seemed pretty mature."

Holcomb also made it clear he was willing to put the work in to become a driver. Because virtually no one grows up near a bobsled track in America, almost everyone comes into the sport as a push athlete, and as we've seen, one can come out of nowhere and make the Olympic team as a push athlete. But it's nigh impossible to do that as a driver. It can take 6 to 10 years of steady improvement to be one of the best in the world. Holcomb says he knew he was ready for that long haul. "I wanted to compete a lot longer, and I had a lot more to give to the sport," Holcomb says. "And honestly and selfishly, if you are a good driver, it's much harder to get beat out by a new young stud. That happens to push athletes all the time." At the end of the 2002-2003 season, Holcomb finished 10th in the World Championships in Lake Placid, in basically his first year as a 4-man pilot. Hays' team had a fantastic Championships and finished with a silver medal — the best U.S. showing in the World Championships since 1959 — showing the gulf between Holcomb and Hays at that point. But Holcomb was on his way. And while Mesler internalized that he probably would never become a driver, the silver lining for him was that he and Holcomb had forged an unbreakable bond.

Despite the overall success of the Bo-Dyn sleds at the Salt Lake City Games, one unfortunate byproduct of Todd Hays finishing higher than any American Olympic bobsledder since 1956 was that the polarizing Hays took his silver medal as a license to promote his vision of U.S. bobsledding. Hays was by his natural confidence very convincing and persuasive, with an uncanny knack for getting teammates to follow him.

Now, with an Olympic silver medal, he was even more able to persuade fellow athletes to see things his way, which included constantly downplaying the effectiveness of the Bo-Dyn sleds. But the Bo-Dyn Project team members knew Hays; they saw how he operated on and off the mountain. It was common knowledge that while Hays fancied himself a bobsled design savant, the truth was that he rarely tinkered with his own sled, much less possessed the talent to bring an original vision to bobsled design. Briglia saw this firsthand many different times traveling with the athletes in Europe. "You know he thought he knew a lot about everything, but he wasn't interested in getting down and working with the sleds," says Frank Briglia. "And that's where we always got more speed out of the sleds, with the kind of adjustments you make in NASCAR."

The irony that Hayes owed his prominence to the fact that he had medaled in Salt Lake City *in a Bo-Dyn sled* was not lost on Bodine and Cuneo. "The way he could lead the athletes like the Pied Piper was pretty amazing because nobody really liked him," says Cuneo. "But Todd had an ability to win people over to his side when it came to taking sides on an issue, even when the facts were not on his side. Clearly our sleds had made a huge impact for Todd and others, but that didn't stop him from trying to sabotage us."

Even as Holcomb was making the transition to the driver, another piece was starting to fall in place for what would become Holcomb's Night Train team in the years ahead. As we've previously seen in the case of everyone from Shimer to Holcomb to Mesler, bobsledding recruiting doesn't follow any standard pattern; it's not like there's an annual draft. So everyone takes their own path, as did Curt Tomasevicz.

A just-graduated football player for the Nebraska Cornhuskers, Tomasevicz was killing time by working out at odd hours in the football weight room in the summer of 2004, keeping in shape as he embarked on a Master's degree in electrical engineering. One day, Nebraska's strength and conditioning coach introduced him to Amanda Morley, a member of the women's national bobsled team. Morley encouraged Tomasevicz to reach out to Latour, who had since become the men's bobsled coach. After absolutely killing the six-point test, Tomasevicz flew up to Calgary in September 2004. Tomasevicz didn't know the timing of the U.S bobsled schedule, but he was trying out extremely late in the winnowing process, as the national team would be having their selection races in late October and early November. In Calgary, he sprinted, lifted weights, and performed tests measuring his natural explosiveness. "It was similar to when I first got to Nebraska for football," Tomasevicz says today. "With the exception that in football, you don't learn how to most efficiently push a 450-pound bobsled."

Tomasevicz's athleticism impressed the coaches. Moreover, he was just the kind of sprinter whose specific style of running was transferrable to bobsledding. One of the reasons NFL superstars like Walker had failed years before was that pure speed isn't all that's needed in bobsledding. The start is like a long-form ballet, with everyone's pacing and stride having to be in concert. The 2-man event is one thing, but coordinating the footwork and entry into a 4-man sled is quite another. "There's kind of a running style, a running technique, that you need to push a bobsled," he says. "A lot of great sprinters don't make good bobsledders because they don't have that particular technique."

Tomasevicz says that when pushing a bobsled, athletes should have their feet on the ground as much as possible, to avoid slipping. He calls it "long ground contact time." A classic sprinter, conversely, will hit the ground and try to get off the ground as quickly as possible. The other element that makes an excellent push athlete is the explosive power needed to push the sled while going from a standstill to a sprint. Power is centered in the core muscles, and one of the best ways to measure core strength is a standing vertical jump. How high someone can jump is an expression of how quickly that person can move his body weight. Tomasevicz' vertical leap was about 40 inches, good enough back at Nebraska to set the record for Cornhusker running backs and linebackers.

So, while many casual observers think that tremendous raw speed is all that's needed to succeed in bobsledding, the best athletes possess a rare blend of speed, power, and a particular sprint technique. "I think of it as we have to be in the top 5% of sprinters, the top 5% of weightlifters, and then we also need that technique," Tomasevicz says. "So the combination of those three characteristics is pretty unique."

Not only did Tomasevicz have the skillset, but he also had impeccable timing. After proving a quick learner in Calgary, he was slotted in right away with Holcomb on the USA-2 2-man sled. Tomasevicz had to pinch himself: in September, he was lifting weights at his alma mater and by December, he had a new career as a bobsledder, teamed with a man who would go on to become the most decorated bobsled pilot in U.S history. "A lot of things fell into place pretty quickly for me, so I was very fortunate," Tomasevicz says.

Tomasevicz, though, wasn't on USA-2 with Holcomb every week. As the newbie on the team, Tomasevicz was quickly introduced to the pragmatic bobsled hierarchy that had long ruled the sport. To have the best chance to win medals on the World Cup circuit every year and then every four years in the Olympics, countries understandably want their very best athletes competing together as a team, and will do whatever it takes to make sure that team is as strong as it can be.

That means that the number two sleds in both the 4-man and 2-man competitions exist as tools, if you will, to see how athletes are progressing, and if they are ready to make the jump to the number one sled, which is the sled that is supposed to bring home the hardware. Holcomb's USA-2 sled, then, was a proving ground and its primary function was not to win, but to promote the best performers to USA-1. "Being on USA-2 in the 2-man, it can change week to week," Tomasevicz says. "So USA-2 is kind of where change happens. One week, I was on with Holkie; the next one, I wouldn't leave the hut at the top of the hill."

For Tomasevicz, that first winter in 2004-2005 was a revelation. "Here I was, having graduated from Nebraska just a few months before, and I was representing the United States as an athlete, traveling around in the Italian Alps," Tomasevicz says. "It's an unbelievable feeling to be traveling around Europe for the first time like that. Sometimes I didn't believe it. But there were also times when I wondered what I was doing there."

And when were those times? Those were the times Tomasevicz would be stuck in a snow storm, on his stomach laying on the cold ground, putting chains on a vehicle's tires so the team could transport their bobsleds up a mountain.

Those were the times he and Holcomb would wander the streets of a European ski resort, unable to buy anything more than a baguette and a Coke because the food was so expensive and their meal money was gone. Those were the times he wasn't making any progress as a bobsledder because someone else was the brakeman for Holcomb.

There was one rock, however, for Tomasevicz and his teammates to cling to. Tomasevicz remembers Frank Briglia as a constant on the circuit, staying late at the track long after everyone else had left and working out in the cold, preparing the sleds between heats as the athletes stayed warm inside. "We might be inside warming up, but Frank was always out there for hours, tinkering with the equipment, watching the other countries race, trying to find an advantage for us," says Tomasevicz. "I think he and Bob Cuneo are the unsung heroes of American bobsledding."

Chapter Seven

The Bodine Challenge:
A New Dawn for the Project

A S TIME WENT on, Tomasevicz, along with Holcomb, started to feel a kinship with the other athletes, party fueled by the goodwill that the Bo-Dyn program was spreading, as Briglia helped other national teams work on their sleds when he could. Weekend after weekend, they found themselves in small mountain towns with the same traveling circus of athletes, coaches, team administrative employees, bobsled officials, and members of the media. For Tomasevicz, even though he was chasing glory for the U.S. in American- made Bo-Dyn sleds, off the mountain the camaraderie extended to his competitors. "After a while, you realize that these guys are no different from you, just from another country and maybe speaking another language," Tomasevicz says. What Tomasevicz was starting to realize was that he actually had more in common with many of his fiercest competitors than he did with 22-year-olds back in the States: a shared penchant for hurtling down a mountain at 70 mph in a sled.

Like all U.S. bobsledders, Tomasevicz also had to worry about making ends meet. But in an illustration of what makes Olympic sports so special, his small Nebraska hometown held a fundraiser for him in June 2005 with a golf tournament and a Main Street talent contest on a flatbed truck smack in the middle of the village. A band played on the truck trailer, and the whole crowd danced into the night. The event raised $25,000 for Tomasevicz. "You know, in the middle of Nebraska where no one had ever seen a bobsled in person, that kind of support is pretty incredible," Tomasevicz says. "They believed in me because I believed in something."

Regarding results, the World Cup circuit in 2004 and 2005 fell into a familiar pattern. Todd Hays was driving USA-1 and Holcomb piloted USA-2. Hays followed up the silver medal he had earned at the previous 4-man World Championships in Lake Placid with bronze in the 4-man World Championships at the end of the 2003-2004 season in Konigssee, Germany. He also took home numerous World

Cup circuit medals in both the 2003-2004 and 2004-2005 seasons. In the year leading up to the 2006 Winter Olympics in Torino, in fact, Hays was regarded as one of the favorites in the 4-man.

Holcomb, meanwhile, earned a bunch of top 10s in those seasons, but no wins. As the 2005 season ended, Holcomb had improved immeasurably but had still never medaled, finishing just off the podium with a couple of 4th place finishes. He did have a solid 4-man team developed with Tomasevicz, Bill Schuffenhauer, and Lorenzo Smith — the team he would take into the 2006 Torino Games.

Mesler, meanwhile, was part of Hays' team and decided to make the best of his mercurial driver's approach. Mesler describes video sessions in which Hays would spot, say, a push athlete whose shoulder would be an inch too high during training. In training, bobsledders typically don't have their race suits on and are wearing more layers, making it hard to hunker all the way down in the bobsled to the normal racing position. But Hays would not have any of that. According to Mesler: "Instead of saying, "Hey, take a look at your shoulders; is there a way to get lower?' Todd would be more like a football coach, swearing and yelling at you. But I will say that I learned from Todd the tenacity and the attention to detail it takes to make those around you better. I was just able to take that intensity and make it more positive, and that was something I was able to take to the Night Train team a few years later."

In the summer of 2005, three future members of the Night Train ended up training together. Holcomb and Tomasevicz came to train in Calgary while Hays and Mesler were also there. As in all things with bobsled, financing was an issue; but, in this instance, there was a silver lining. Mesler had a house that he was leasing, and he let Tomasevicz sleep on the couch that summer, so they could all save money, in exchange for some sweat equity help around the house. "That's how I got to know Curt; and I'd already known Holcomb, of course, being that it was a pretty close team," Mesler says. "So the three of us hung out that summer and hit it off. But during those weeks in Calgary, you could also see that Holcomb threatened Hays."

Hays, in fact, was up to his old tricks. For some time, he had been lobbying the USBSF and its president, Bob Pokelwaldt – who had taken over shortly after the Salt Lake City Games — for support to fund his own ideas concerning sled technology, even while he continued to use Bo-Dyn sleds. The much-respected Pokelwaldt was the recently retired

Chief Operating Officer of York International and, according to John Morgan, the "most competent person ever to be in charge of U.S. bobsledding." Attorney Dan Goodwin, who was on the USBSF Board at the time, puts it this way: "Todd Hays had this idea that, 'Why should this money from the USOC go to Bo-Dyn by way of the USBSF? I can build a better mousetrap.'" In July 2005, Hays requested a Bo-Dyn chassis to assemble his own bobsled. That same month, USA bobsled marketing executive and Hays ally, Terry Kent, went to the USBSF Board of Directors annual meeting in Lake Placid to ask if it would consider funding Hays' idea for an aerodynamic cowling, along with a Bo-Dyn chassis that he could fit it on. Garrett Hines, push athlete on Hays' silver medal sled in Salt Lake City who was an athlete representative on the USBSF Board, also got in on the act, making a presentation on behalf of Hays (who wasn't in the room) to the USBSF on why the Board should support Hays. His argument was that he and Hays had already finished second in the 4-man competition at the Salt Lake Games and did not want to do it again. Hays had dangled a return spot on his sled if Hines supported him, but Hines ended up never getting that spot. The irony here is that Hays and Hines had finished 4th in the 2-man at the Salt Lake Games, just a few hundredths of a second out of bronze, and if it were not for a start mishap between the two of them in one of the heats, they would have won that historic first medal.

Cuneo and Briglia suspected that Hays eventually wanted to sell his own bobsleds after he retired from the sport and, subsequently, advised the USBSF that it objected to Hays' request out of concerns that its intellectual property would be stolen by Hays for use in his future bobsleds. And how did the Bo-Dyn team voice its objection? Cuneo told the Executive Board of the USBSF that if it went ahead and gave Hays access to a Bo-Dyn chassis, he would make a big pile of Bo-Dyn bobsleds in the parking lot of the USOC training center in Lake Placid and destroy them in a huge bonfire! It was a strategy one might label as "scorched earth." The USBSF's answer? They voted to deny Hays' request for the Bo-Dyn chassis.

In response, Hines led a no-confidence vote against Pokelwaldt one week later, positing that Pokelwaldt was holding back the building of a better sled than the Bo-Dyn sleds. The no-confidence vote passed by one vote. "I think part of the problem with a lot of those Board members was that they kowtowed to the athletes," Goodwin says. "These people were volunteer amateurs who just wanted to put this on their resumes." Pokelwaldt, to his credit, said to the athletes, 'Leave the business part to us. You guys are the athletes; train and do your best on the track, and leave the management to us.' But these young athletes would follow Hays through a brick wall. He was the reigning silver medalist. He was king."

After the close vote, Pokelwaldt resigned in mid-August, much to the dismay of Goodwin and the Bo-Dyn team, all of whom viewed Pokelwaldt as one of the few adults in the room when it came to the USBSF Board. Cuneo, understandably, was getting more and more fed up with defending the Bo-Dyn sleds from Hays and his fellow Bo-Dyn detractors. "Cuneo was disenchanted at this point," Morgan says. After the Hays group had won the no-confidence vote, even Cuneo himself thought he had had enough; in fact, he had mentioned to Morgan on some occasions that this would be his last year involved with the project.

Goodwin and finance executive John Vester, both USBSF Executive Board members and both of whom would later also serve a crucial role on the Bo-Dyn Board, experienced from their insiders' perch just how dysfunctional the 21-member USBSF Board was. But after thinking long and hard about what course of action they should take after the no-confidence vote, both decided that for the time being, they were better off working as members of the Board and not resigning, lest they be accused of leaving simply out of sour grapes. Instead, they started to try to convince the USOC that the USBSF was being ruled by the inmates – in this case, athletes Hays and Hines.

Politics aside, there were some positive developments in that spring and summer of 2005, and – as always seemed the case with the Bo-Dyn Project – new ideas jolted things back to life just when energy was needed most.

By mid-2005, the financial side of the Bo-Dyn Project was, as was often the case, running on fumes, particularly with the political battles raging within the USBSF Board about the level of support that should be given to the Bo-Dyn Project. The World Cup wins weren't coming fast enough to draw in new, deep-pocket sponsors, and money was needed to refurbish the sleds to get them in tip-top condition for the Olympics in Torino the next year. In May 2005, John Morgan finally accepted Geoff Bodine's longstanding offer to attend a NASCAR event and attended the annual All-Star weekend usually the week before the NASCAR Memorial Day weekend race in Concord, NC. During the festivities, Morgan essentially told Bodine that he feared the Bo-Dyn Project was dying a slow death. Morgan was a man who had big ideas, and he told Bodine that the project, now in its second decade, needed a really big idea to get to the next level.

The first question Bodine had for Morgan concerned what, exactly, had to be done: What did Morgan suggest? Morgan responded that the USBSF had not capitalized on the Salt Lake Games success three years earlier. His radical concept was that they needed NASCAR drivers in bobsleds. Morgan understood that from Day One back in 1992 when Bodine had decided to build Made in America sleds, that the Bo-Dyn's project's biggest ideas and innovations had always been NASCAR related. It made sense to more overtly make that connection to NASCAR and put celebrated NASCAR drivers into the drivers' seats of bobsleds. The second question Bodine had for Morgan was: *How* do we do that?

Morgan's answer was to create the Geoff Bodine Bobsled Challenge. Race car drivers would be brought up to Lake Placid and have a great time trying to beat each other down the mountain. Yes, race car drivers, in the middle of winter, before their NASCAR racing season started, would be asked to come up to upstate New York and drive bobsleds.

Bodine loved the idea, so Morgan went next to Kurze. Kurze knew of Morgan's involvement with the sport as both a broadcaster and TV Production company, of course, and still had memories of his fraternity brother from the early 1970s at college, taking breaks from his rugby games to tell anyone who would listen that when the Olympics came back to Lake Placid in 1980, he was going to make his mark at the Games. "We all said, 'Sure, we'll see you at the Olympics,'" Kurze and their other fraternity brothers would kid Morgan. But sure enough, Morgan not only made a decent showing with his brothers at the 1980 Olympic bobsled trials but also started his own production company and sports marketing business while still competing in the sport. "No one was more connected to the U.S. team, or to bobsledding itself, as John Morgan," Kurze says. "It was great that in 2005, John was coming off the sidelines as mainly a commentator to see if he could make some things happen."

None of the three were deterred by the logistical challenges. They were convinced that tapping into NASCAR fans' enthusiasm for their stars, together with the natural competitiveness of race car drivers, would make the idea work and bring in some major sponsors and basic support from the companies who support NASCAR. In July 2005, the Geoff Bodine Bobsled Challenge was officially created with the goal of getting NASCAR drivers to compete in a bobsled race to promote the sport to the NASCAR community. "You have to remember," Geoff Bodine says, "race car drivers are nuts. I've raced just about every kind of vehicle. But it doesn't have to be a vehicle. I would race to see who can get to the refrigerator first. These guys were not going to resist going to the Geoff Bodine Bobsled Challenge."

There was the not-so-small matter, however, of the sleds. Sleds would need to be built for the Bodine Challenge because the Bo-Dyn sleds were in use, of course. It was clear that the expertise of Cuneo and his team at Chassis Dynamics wasn't affordable; in fact, it wasn't needed. These sleds just had to get the NASCAR drivers down the track in one piece; no one was vying for an Olympic medal with them. Morgan and Kurze settled on a man named Don Hass to build the ten sleds. Hass' design firm had previously built youth sleds and could build a functional Bodine Challenge fleet of ten sleds for $10,000 apiece. With Whelen coming through with the first check for funding for the sleds, the biggest hurdle to the Bodine Challenge becoming a reality was overcome. The first promotional theme that the Challenge used was the "Made in America" premise of the Bo-Dyn Project itself.

Since the Bo-Dyn Project was now thinking bigger, Morgan and Kurze designed a budget to match that ambition.

The Bo-Dyn Project Board – now with Morgan as executive director — developed in late 2005 a five-year business plan, noting that the fleet of Bo-Dyn bobsleds had chassis that averaged about ten years of age. They staked out a goal of building the "sled of the future" that could be showcased at the 2010 Vancouver Games. Morgan set out a $5 million budget that included $2 million for sled design and $2 million for athlete and coach development/administration, so that great push athletes who could eventually develop into great pilots could continue to be recruited. But the limited funding from the USBSF and USOC were barely enough for year-to-year sled maintenance, and even the Whelen sponsorship couldn't begin to fund this ambitious plan. That's where the Bodine Challenge and, hopefully, the slew of new sponsorships it would attract, came in.

The first-ever Challenge was held on the weekend of January 7-8, 2006, and sponsors included Whelen, Chevrolet, the I Love NY tourism initiative, and Columbia Sportswear. Hendrick Motorsports provided the private plane that flew all of the drivers from Concord, North Carolina to Lake Placid. According to Bodine, Rick Hendrick's plane was one of the main reasons that the Challenge attracted so many drivers. "There were guys who didn't know they were going up to

Lake Placid until the day the plane left," Bodine says. "If you were down in that area, you'd jump on the plane, and they flew you at no charge. We couldn't have even had the event without that plane." Hendrick wanted no exposure and only wanted to support the driver who won Hendrick Motorsports first-ever NASCAR Cup win in 1985 and their first Daytona 500 victory in 1986—Bodine.

Columbia Sports provided winter clothes for all of the NASCAR drivers, some of whom just threw on a light coat in Charlotte for the flight up north. We're not talking about a pair of ear muffs here, either, but coats, hats, gloves, boots, everything the drivers – not to mention their families if they came along — would need to hang around the North Country for a cold winter weekend. It was -5 when they departed the airplane at the Saranac Lake Regional Airport 15 miles from Lake Placid. Bodine remembers whole families being outfitted, with John Morgan calling people over and saying, "C'mon, did you get a jacket? We have jackets your size." "Columbia gave away huge amounts of clothing," Bodine says. "I had to tell John, 'Okay, that's too much. You have to stop. Everyone has two of everything.'" Morgan's goal, above all else, was to treat the NASCAR driver and their families like kings, to encourage more of them to participate so that the event would grow. It worked. "The whole town treated the NASCAR guys like celebrities, treated them very, very well," Morgan says. And that's why they kept coming back."

Morgan organized coverage on ESPN2 and the Speed Channel and produced the program with a Bo-Dyn "Made in America" theme. Because there was concern that the sleds might not perform to the liking of a NASCAR driver, the event was recorded and shown several weeks later. The four hours of television that aired on ESPN2 and the Speed Channel received respectable viewing numbers, and the drivers made it down the track in one piece, which was another concern.

Morgan and his team also decided to let the media take a spin down the track in the sleds, with one reporter writing in his story published in the *New York Times* that it was the "ride of a lifetime." "The kind of coverage we got was something you can't even buy," says Phil Kurze. "The Bodine Challenge put us in the conversation in so many places we wouldn't have been." The NASCAR media covered the event and used it as programming to show a different side of race car drivers. For example, many different NASCAR-related television productions used video clips provided by Bo-Dyn in the run-up to, and on the day of, the 2006 Daytona 500 race. Chevrolet requested one of the sleds to be shipped to the

Daytona 500, where media and spectators had a chance to sit in the sled on the infield of the track.

The roster of NASCAR drivers who attended that first Bodine Challenge, just a month before the 2006 Torino Games, included Bodine and his brother, Todd Bodine, Randy LaJoie, Dick Trickle, and Boris Said, among others. "This was without a doubt the coolest charity event I've ever been involved with," Said says. "I mean, think of receiving this pitch: You can play golf all day or go down a mountain at 75 miles per hour. For this crowd, that was an easy choice." Said describes how, at the beginning of the weekend, the drivers would begin at Start 5, the spot closest to the bottom of the track. After a couple of runs at Start 5, they moved them to Start 3. From Start 3, they could get some serious speed going. And they loved it! "I wanted to win," says Boris Said, a driver who attended all of the Bodine Challenges. "I mean, all of us are very competitive. We all wanted to win!"

He won both races contested that first year, but that didn't mean he wasn't scared. According to him, "Bobsledding is one crazy, crazy sport. You cannot believe the acceleration these sleds have. You're going 60 or 70 miles per hour, but it seems like you are going 500. It's just an incredible thrill. It's the fastest thing I've ever been in without a motor." Said knows of what he speaks; his father was a driver on the USA Olympic Bobsled Team in 1968 and 1972.

One of the aspects of the Challenge that the NASCAR racers liked was that they were bringing some attention to their fellow racers, even if it was racing on ice. "These athletes train 24/7, 365 days a year; and they get very little limelight," Said explains. "It was the least we could do to bring some attention to them and try to help them." Said, an entrepreneur who owns a series of go-cart tracks, even welcomed a whole contingent of Team USA bobsledders who were doing some offseason training at the Chula Vista Olympic Training Center in Southern California out to one of his go-cart tracks in San Diego for some fun, followed by a seminar about the similarities between race car driving and bobsledding.

Said was one of the few race cars drivers who took to bobsledding immediately in Lake Placid that weekend. Said – who participated in all five Challenges – never crashed. Only Joey Logano, who attended his first Challenge at age 17, could also claim to have never crashed, although he didn't participate until the second year of the event. "You know why bobsled drivers are always out of breath when they are at the bottom of a hill?" asks Said. "Because it's so intense, you don't breathe — you just hold your breath the whole time. But, yes, luckily I never turned one over. It just suited me." Said was so good that he was invited by Team USA to drive a real 2-man Bo-Dyn sled, which handles much better than the test sleds built for the Bodine Challenges. "The articulation on those sleds is incredible," he says. "It's like a Kia compared to a BMW M5. Completely different."

To make the starts equal, former three-time Olympic bobsled athlete, the late Phil "Brown Bear" Duprey, pushed the sled to a painted line. This was not about the push or the start; it was about the driving. The race drivers were joined in their sleds by National Guardsmen to occupy the second spot in the 2-man sleds. Since the team wasn't doing any pushing, it didn't matter who occupied the brakeman spot. Unfortunately, though, some of the guardsmen got a little beat up as many drivers weren't as successful as Said keeping the bobsleds upright. "Yeah, they might not have anticipated that particular assignment when they signed on with the National Guard," says Said with a laugh.

The race car drivers loved the Bodine Challenge for a lot of reasons that went beyond winning, losing, or how good they were at handling the sleds. In the midst of a NASCAR season, there's not a lot of time to be social. From joking around on the plane up to Lake Placid to going out to the local watering holes in the Olympic Village, it was a great pre-season treat for NASCAR drivers. The camaraderie was special. Here they could yuck it up, compete, but not worry around who won or lost. Not only was the event successful regarding exposure for the Bo-Dyn Project, but after the first year, other big sponsors wanted to get involved in the Challenge or donate to the Bo-Dyn Project, among them Lucas Oil and JEGS, which is a racing equipment company.

Another positive of the Challenge is that it improved the morale of "Team Provolone," who all attended the event. Cuneo, in particular, was energized when he learned that Whelen would pay him a monthly engineering fee guaranteed. He would not have to worry about not getting paid anymore.

With the Bodine Challenge a great success and the success of Hays and – to a lesser extent – Holcomb as drivers, everything pointed to a big Olympic Games in Torino for the Team USA bobsled squad, even considering the political troubles that Hays had instigated within the USFBF. All that was to be set aside for the good of Team USA so that Hays and Holcomb could drive their Bo-Dyn sleds the way they knew how. Surely, Torino was where USA men's bobsledding would finally bring home gold with a Bo-Dyn sled.

On the track, Hays continued as one of the strongest drivers on the circuit. Just a couple weeks after the Bodine Challenge, Hays won the 4-man event in St. Moritz. As February approached, everyone was ready. But a pall was cast over the Olympics for the U.S. even before the Games began. Sexual harassment accusations were made against the national skeleton team coach, who was fired by the USOC, through the barely functioning USBSF, the Saturday before the Games were to begin. Once again, off-track challenges presented by the USBSF would hinder the Bo-Dyn Project, which was no different from the previous three Olympics.

It didn't take long, however, for the U.S. women to change the narrative with another bravura Olympic performance. Just as in Salt Lake City, they came through and made more history driving Bo-Dyn sleds. Shauna Rohbock, a former professional soccer player, won the women's silver medal with push athlete Valerie Fleming.

In the men's 2-man, one of the hundreds of little things that can go wrong on the bobsled track struck Holcomb and his brakeman Bill Schuffenhauer in the first heat. They clipped a wall and bent the push bar, ruining the aerodynamics of the sled. Overall, Holcomb had what he describes as "just a bad day," and he and Schuffenhauer were mired in 14th place and would finish out of the medal hunt in 13th place. Hays and brakeman, Pavle Jovanovic, were the pair everyone was watching, however, and they could only manage a 7th -place finish.

It was the marquee 4-man event, though, that would change the trajectory of U.S. bobsledding for the next decade. A couple of months before the Olympics, a USBSF bobsled official had approached Holcomb and told him that the 2005-2006 season was going to be critical for him. USA-1, driven by Hays, had won multiple World Cup race medals in the past few years, and he had not won any. "They pulled me aside," Holcomb says. "Basically they told me they just couldn't put more money into a losing team and that they couldn't keep supporting me if the performance wasn't there." Holcomb knew these Games were his last, best chance to hold onto his spot.

Medal favorite, Hays, and his team were just one spot ahead of Holcomb after the first heat, and then a great run by Holcomb in the second heat left his sled one ahead of Hays, in 6th place. Even though Hays' push athletes, Mesler, Pavle Jovanovic, and Brock Kreitzburg, were giving their driver great start times, Hays was losing time down the track. Following the day's racing, something happened that shocked everyone and still has coaches and athletes shaking their heads ten years later. After his second heat, Hays made a statement to the media:

> *"Tomorrow will be my last two bobsled runs,*
> *and you'll see every ounce of energy that I have*
> *in this sport. Unfortunately, it didn't go as I'd*
> *hoped; but, fortunately, I know there are a lot*
> *worse things in life than not finishing the*
> *Olympic Games with a medal."*

Hays hadn't performed the way he wanted; and, even though his sled was still well within striking distance of a medal, he had essentially retired from the sport in the middle of the competition. His push athletes, confused, had no idea what to think. They wanted to go out and win the next day, but they were pushing for a man who actually retired during what served as the "halftime" of their sport. Everyone could palpably feel Hays wilting the next day in the shadow of Holcomb as the Hays sled slipped to 10th after the third heat, ultimately finishing 7th to Holcomb's 6th place. After he had finished, Hays slipped on some sweat pants and watched the rest of the race from the track. There were no shaking hands with Holcomb, or even a "see you later." According to Dan Goodwin, Hays' move epitomized the man perfectly. "It created shockwaves through the U.S. team," Goodwin says. "It perfectly showed his volatility and how he was the master of the unpredictable."

For the men, the disappointment of not medaling with Bo-Dyn sleds was mollified by the fact that a new USA-1 was baptized. "It was huge for me," Holcomb says. "I'm still pretty green at this point in 2006, remember. I haven't won any medals, have just finished fourth a few times. After that, I just put my head down and went for it."

After the Olympics, the USOC, as was its wont, took stock and did an evaluation of all of the different winter sports federations, and their gaze fell on the USBSF. Between the skeleton sexual harassment scandal, the political mess that was the USBSF Board, and the under-performance of its top entry in the 4-man, the decision was made by the USOC to disband the USBSF Board on March 1, 2006, and ask for the resignations of all its members.

The carnage at the USBSF Board was, talent-wise, a boon for the Bo-Dyn Project Board. A meeting was scheduled at Whelen Engineering just a few weeks after the Torino games, and the USOC announcement of disbanding the USBSF Board. The meeting was attended by Kurze, Morgan, Bodine and Cuneo.

First, Kurze, Morgan, and Bodine discussed that the Bo-Dyn Board needed to be infused with some new blood; and Morgan suggested Goodwin and Vester. Between their technical expertise in law and finance, respectively, their history with the sport, and their experience interacting with the USOC representing the USBSF, there weren't two people on earth who could bring more valuable skills to the Bo-Dyn Board at that point than Goodwin and Vester. Dialed into the meeting by speaker phone, the two – both of whom had a history with Morgan — agreed to be on the Board, even though neither one had ever met Kurze. The newfound Bo-Dyn Board of Directors would need legal help, and with an attorney on the Board, Dan Goodwin took care of that. Yale graduate Vester, who had himself had been a member of the USA Luge Team, worked in the financial services industry and would be perfect for the Treasurer position. "They were both very energetic and had a bad taste in their mouths from what had happened with all the politics in the United States Bobsled Federation in the past," Kurze says. "So it was the best of both worlds; they knew the sport, they knew the

USBSF, and they had the talents we needed. And they were both great guys."

Morgan and Kurze also wanted it to be easier to raise funds via donations, given that they were hoping that the Bo-Dyn Project would soon have a much higher profile. It was decided at the meeting that the Bo-Dyn Board would try to qualify for not-for-profit corporation status as a Connecticut State Corporation. That way, potential donors interested in the project's patriotic message could make a contribution and have it be tax-deductible. "It sounds like a small thing," Kurze said. "But it was a big selling point." Ed Flink, the lawyer from Lake Placid who also attended the meeting, was able to achieve not-for-profit status of the Board within a couple of months of the meeting.

With the USBSF Board disbanded, the Bo-Dyn Board reinvigorated, Hays retired, and a new USA-1 taking flight, even Cuneo was heartened. "We were ready to take off," Cuneo says. "With the USBSF Board in place, we could never have done what came next." With no onerous Board to deal with, Cuneo and company just had to make the sleds go as fast as they could. Newly liberated, Cuneo was playing around with the idea that would launch Holcomb and his team into a season never before experienced by an American bobsledder.

Chapter Eight

Independence Day

SUMMER IS VACATION time for millions of Americans, as it was for Bob Cuneo in 2006.

It was planned as a fun trip to the Pacific Northwest for Cuneo and his wife to visit their three children — a son, a daughter, and an adopted daughter — who had moved to the Seattle area. They would go to Pike Place Market, take the elevator up to the viewing deck of the Space Needle, stop by the Seattle Aquarium — just do all of those things residents, such as their kids, might never get around to.

The second part of the trip involved renting a big Suburban and heading north to Canada to enjoy Vancouver and Whistler. But Cuneo being Cuneo, there was a work angle, too. Heck, Cuneo being Cuneo, maybe the work angle *was* the reason for the vacation, and the kids were just a plausible excuse. A man named Craig Lehto was the track director at Whistler Sliding Center, then under construction for the 2010 Vancouver Games. Cuneo got hold of Lehto and asked if he could come to see the construction site, and Lehto responded that he'd be more than happy to show Cuneo around.

That's how Cuneo became the first person not affiliated with the Canadian bobsled team to witness first-hand the progress that was being made on the track. It was still early days for the construction, but as Cuneo walked the hill (low to high, of course), he could see the forms for the concrete and the steep drops that defined what would be the final track. According to Cuneo: "I thought to myself, 'Holy shit, is this going to be fast.' I knew I saw it before anyone. So the wheels started turning. When I got back to Connecticut, I said to everyone, 'Okay, we have to think about how to build the right sled for this track.'" Cuneo's goal was to build the perfect sled for what he thought just might be the fastest track in the world.

Seeing the Vancouver Olympic site only added to the sense of urgency Cuneo felt in 2006 to go back to the drawing board with his Chassis Dynamics team. In fact, for some reasons, Cuneo felt under more pressure than ever to come up with the goods. First, the implosion of the USBSF Board and the successful first Bodine Challenge meant that the political obstacles had been cleared away and the financial picture was a bit more positive. So the Bo-Dyn Project had a new lease on life to try and come up with the next generation of Bo-Dyn sleds. That was on Cuneo and his team.

Second, since the shocking mid-Olympics retirement in Torino of former USA pilot, Todd Hays, Hays had been trying to develop bobsleds for sale on the open market, eyeing foreign rivals of the United States. Cuneo, understandably, wanted to make sure that his sleds were better than any Hays' product out there. Third, Hays had stirred up the pot to such an extent that Cuneo was still angry that several USBSF Board members joined Hays in his crusade against the Bo-Dyn Project. He wouldn't mind putting those people in their place, even though the Board was, at that point, defunct.

Lastly (and perhaps most importantly), the elusive men's gold medal had not yet materialized. No one came right out and said it to the Bo-Dyn engineering and design team, but after four Olympics, it was surely disappointing that the Bo-Dyn medal count didn't include a men's Olympic gold medal. And, yes, the women's gold in 2002 was a huge, historic accomplishment, and an achievement with which the

Bo-Dyn Project would always be associated. But the men's 4-man is *the* event of Olympic bobsledding, and even though Geoff Bodine professed complete satisfaction in how his original vision had been executed — "Bob, and Frank, and everyone else have already taken the U.S. so far from where we were" was a typical comment he would make to the sports media — Bodine's magnanimity didn't change the fact that there was a major hole in the Bo-Dyn Olympic resume.

As Cuneo considered the most likely areas of improvement for the sleds, he kept turning over in his mind the steering mechanism, an engineering element that had been pretty much settled years earlier. Cuneo and Vaillancourt at the beginning of the Bo-Dyn Project, and then Briglia later on, had all tinkered in their own way with the steering until the athletes were in basic agreement that both the 2-man and the 4-man sleds were handling very well.

Still, in recent years the pilots would occasionally provide feedback that the 2and 4-man driving experiences were markedly different. As if the weather and track variables from event to event were not enough to factor in, the drivers also had to adjust from the 2-man to the 4-man races regarding how the sleds responded to the steering input. The different lengths and weight of the 2- and 4-man sleds made the handling of the sleds very different. Cuneo had more than once thought to himself that if there were a way he could align the steering systems to create the same "feel" in the 2-man and 4-man for Holcomb and the other drivers, they would have an advantage over their competitors, because it would seem as if they were practicing and competing with one set of steering responses.

One might wonder why that would be such an advantage; after all, how hard is it to learn to handle just two sleds? Golfers, for example, have *14* different clubs to master. But during race week on the World Cup bobsled circuit, there is a limited number of practice runs down the hill.

The schedule typically goes something like this: Race days are Saturday and Sunday. On Sunday night everyone loads up their sleds and drives on to the next site; hotels are checked into, and any rudimentary language skills applicable to the new locale are dusted off. On Monday, all the equipment is unloaded and organized. Tuesday is devoted to 2-man practice, and each team gets two runs down the hill. The 4-man sleds take center stage on Wednesdays, with each team squeezing in two 4-man runs. The final practice day is Thursday, the last window for a couple more 2-man runs.

Friday is used as an open day in case weather has set the schedule back during the week. Then race days again on Saturday and Sunday before everyone shoves off to another new locale. If Cuneo could create one steering system, it would mean that a team would essentially be practicing during the week with the same sled six times, getting that much more reps as compared to four 2-man trips and two 4-man trips. "The major question in bobsledding is: How can you eliminate variables so the pilot can replicate the same performance race after race?" Cuneo says. "When it comes to steering, if the 2- and 4-man feel the same, you have a huge advantage."

It was Holcomb who brought the issue to a head, approaching Cuneo and Briglia at the conclusion of the first part of the 2006 World Cup season. Cuneo knew Holcomb must have something important to say because it wasn't Holcomb's style to question the basic engineering of the sleds. While Holcomb would chat plenty with Briglia on the circuit about small adjustments to his sleds, he trusted that the Bo-Dyn designers knew what they were doing. "I relied on Frank do his thing," Holcomb says. "He'd been working on these things for years with Cuneo."

But Holcomb was now the top USA driver; what he said mattered and what he wanted was something that had to be considered. As the new USA-1 pilot on both the 2- and 4-man sleds, Holcomb had started out the 2006-2007 season by shocking the bobsled world, taking silvers in the 2-man in Calgary and Park City, his first medals of any kind. In December 2006, in fact, Holcomb was ranked number one in the World Cup rankings with three 2nd -place finishes in the 2-man. But his 4-man results were not as good and that was when he came to Cuneo and Briglia with a big-picture question: could they possibly find some way to improve his times in the 4-man when the European leg of the circuit started after the Christmas break? "Is there any way we can make these things drive exactly the same?" he asked.

Cuneo took it as a personal challenge to try to minimize the steering differences between the two sleds. He interviewed Holcomb at length about what was working for him in the 2-man as opposed to the 4-man. It turned out that, to Holcomb, the sleds had very distinct feels. The 2-man was akin to a very responsive race car, responding to the slightest steering input from Holcomb on the two metal steering rings. But Holcomb preferred the lagging, or as Cuneo put it, the "lazy" feeling steering response of the 4-

man, which didn't react quite so tightly to Holcomb's steering action. "It wasn't that one was good, and one was bad," Cuneo says. "It was just that they were different, and Steve had a preference."

The challenge for Cuneo was figuring out how he would alter the steering of the 2-man to make it less responsive, making it seem similar to the feel of the slower-reacting 4-man sled. Moreover, he had to adjust the steering in a way that would make it react in a predictable way every time, which requires some knowledge of kinematics, the branch of mechanics that deals with how bodies or objects move through space as they interact with their environment. In other words, the mechanics of keeping something in a straight line – or not – depending on the outside stimulus. "You know, people have this vision that steering in a bobsled is a rope tied to axles," Cuneo says. "Steering is a very sophisticated system. There are levers and pulleys and cams. To understand how it all interacts you have to understand how the machine is going to respond as you tweak the different variables."

Over the break, Cuneo and Briglia hunkered down in Oxford to do a thorough mechanical study of all the different motions that affected the movement of the sleds. The process involved isolating different parts of the 2-man steering, changing a variable, and then measuring the reaction to the steering input. They tried different tweaks to create scores of different scenarios and then painstakingly went through each of them, trying to make the sleds react similarly to steering input.

Finally, in early January, Cuneo and Briglia settled on a combination of adjustments they believed had the sleds reacting reasonably alike. Of course, their tweaks hadn't been tried in a sled being piloted down a bobsled track yet. They put the sleds back together and shipped them off to Cortina, Italy for the start of the European circuit. Holcomb was hopeful but had no idea what to expect.

Now, one thing that had always been true about Cuneo and his colleagues from Chassis Dynamics was that they were their own worst critics. If Cuneo or Briglia thought they had done a decent job on something, the results were nearly always stellar. So it was no surprise when Holcomb tried out the new steering in the 4-man and could not tell the difference between the steering in the 2-man. "It was amazing, but that's sort of what those guys do," Holcomb says. "Some people like a lot of variances and some like a little; some people like a stiff feel to the sled and some like it loose. The NASCAR system they'd put in makes things adjustable. It was great, but honestly, I wasn't surprised."

Holcomb felt in complete control of both sleds in Cortina. Team Holcomb took not only the 2-man gold but the 4-man gold as well. The next week there was another race in Italy, at the Olympic track in Torino. Holcomb went two-for-two again. Four races in Italy after the steering changes, and four wins. "That was pretty cool to sweep Italy," Holcomb says.

The steering system Cuneo implemented might not have been "unique" strictly speaking, but the way it was applied to make both kinds of sleds handle similarly was a singular approach. "With the Bo-Dyn sleds, it was always the case that if you let go of the steering, the sleds always tracked completely straight," says Latour. "They were just that well-engineered. But the biggest thing about the steering changes in 2006 was that they enabled that consistency of performance from the 2-man to the 4-man."

One other factor that might have been affecting Holcomb's 4-man performance in the first half of the 2006-2007 World Cup season was the absence of Tomasevicz. In September 2006, Tomasevicz returned to Lincoln, Nebraska to finish his Masters in electrical engineering. For Tomasevicz, education was crucial, and he didn't anticipate living in a dorm room and surviving on the stipend given to those athletes on USA-1 — about $1,500-2,000 a month — for too many more years. The stipend, along with the $25,000 raised at his hometown fund-raiser the year before, together with some small local sponsorships and speaking engagements, enabled him to make his cell phone and car payments. But Tomasevicz, clearly, already had one eye on his post-bobsled career in 2006.

He rejoined the team for the second half of the 2006-2007 season. Since he hadn't practiced with the 4-man squad and the 4-man is much tougher to choreograph what with four athletes pushing and having to coordinate entry in the sled, Tomasevicz came back primarily as the brakeman on Holcomb's sled. After the Italian sweep, Holcomb and Tomasevicz kept winning. They expected to win every week. "It's hard to say exactly what clicked. But we had fun doing it," Tomasevicz says. Soon, Tomasevicz was back on the 4-man with Brock Kreitzburg and Mesler, who was now also pushing on Holcomb's 4-man sled, with Hays retired.

With the new steering system in place, Holcomb and his push athletes continued to tear up the circuit that winter of 2007. These were the first medals in Holcomb's career, and they came fast and furious. After just 6 stops and 12 races into the season, Holcomb-driven sleds had five golds and three silver medals. Holcomb's 2-man won the World Cup, and the 4-man finished second. At the World Championships in St Moritz, Holcomb finished just off the podium. A sub-par final heat submarined his chance to win a medal in the 4-man where he was only a few hundredths out of the lead going into the 4th run. "Holcomb arrived that season," Cuneo said. "And he arrived because he had worked hard to become a great driver, but he also had an advantage now moving from the 2 to the 4-man regarding the steering. That steering system was the turning point of the project. And if the USBSF were still in charge, it would have never happened, because they wouldn't give us the freedom to experiment the way we did over that Christmas break."

The women were also having an excellent 2006-2007 World Cup season. Rohbock teamed up with Valerie Fleming to take second in the overall World Cup standings, including wins in Calgary and Park City.

The results were so good that in the spring of 2007, the Bo-Dyn Project team was thinking that they might be on the cusp of dominating the sport at least through the next Olympics in Vancouver, and maybe even after that. Given all that had transpired in the past six months, it appeared to the Bo-Dyn Board the perfect time to make the pitch to the USOC to go all-in on the Bo-Dyn Project. After all, the USBSF Board was defunct (a temporary, interim Board had been installed but had little or no power and no collective background in the sport), and the results on the mountain had never been better.

It's important to remember that the United States team was receiving no help from the USBSF for the changes that Cuneo was making or for the refurbishment and maintenance of the 12 bobsled Bo-Dyn fleet. It took a lot of creativity and generosity from different Bo-Dyn sponsors to keep things on track. For example, in 2007, the USBSF Marketing Director Terry Kent approached Bo-Dyn, saying that the team had no winter clothing for the upcoming season. The Bo-Dyn Project parlayed its Columbia Sportswear sponsorship and outfitted the entire men's and women's bobsled and skeleton teams — almost 90 athletes — with outerwear embroidered such that they looked like a NASCAR Team. For Morgan, seeing the teams perfectly outfitted was immensely satisfying, as this was just the kind of first-class treatment that he and others close to him who had devoted their lives to the sport — his brothers, father, and uncle – had never enjoyed.

Meanwhile, Whelen, which was essentially funding the program at this point, could not be expected to write checks into perpetuity. Their generosity was already keeping the project afloat. That spring of 2007, Whelen had given a straight donation of $150,000 to the Bo-Dyn Project, $50,000 of which was designated for research and development which would ultimately become the Night Train. Whelen CEO John Olson, handed the $50,000 check directly to Cuneo, telling him "From one engineer to another, go build the sled of tomorrow." The truth is that throughout the life of the Bo-Dyn Project, Whelen contributed more than the USOC and the USBSF in cash or in-kind donations toward the development and maintenance of the Bo-Dyn bobsleds.

The point being this: the Bo-Dyn Project was long overdue for some direct funding from the USOC. On April 11, 2007, Morgan, Bodine, Cuneo, Goodwin, Vester, Kurze, David Kurtz, and Whelen's James Olson flew out to Colorado Springs on a Whelen aircraft to make their pitch.

Independence Day

While nearly every member of Team USA expresses neutrality when it comes to the behind-the-scenes political battles at the USBSF and the organization's history of mismanagement and disorganization, Holcomb admits to feeling relief when the USBSF finally imploded in March 2006, and the USOC took over. "There were so many chiefs trying to run the place and trying to take over that it was just a shit show," he says. "But as I remember, it was a little confusing what was going to happen next, who or what would fill that vacuum."

That's where the Bo-Dyn Board came in. Now that the sport's inept governing body was sidelined, Morgan, as the Bo-Dyn Executive Director, wanted to make sure they didn't blow their opportunity to get a firm funding commitment from the USOC. Bodine and Cuneo had relationships with USOC from the prior years, but those were more from the technical bobsled creation standpoint. With the USBSF previously acting as the bridge to the USOC, none of the long-time members of the project – Bodine, Cuneo, Kurze or Morgan – had ever had a sit-down with the USOC regarding the Bo-Dyn Project.

Goodwin and Vester, on the other hand, through their torturous years as the sane voices on the USBSF Board, had been involved in various legal and financial meetings with the USOC. They helped prep their fellow Board members regarding how the meeting might go and how aggressive they should be in what they ask for. "Vester and I were the business guys," Goodwin says. "We were the political guys. We were the guys who knew the ins and outs of how the USOC and how the USBSF operated. And we suspected how everything was going to come down at the meeting." With Goodwin's and Vester's input, Morgan crafted the agenda, which included short individual presentations on different topics related to the project Attorney David Kurtz was there as a long-time supporter of the Bo-Dyn Bobsled Project, but he was also the Vice President of Legal Affairs of the FIBT, the sport's world governing body. He and Goodwin had legal input.

Aboard the aircraft on the way to Colorado Springs, the group huddled. What exactly did they want to ask for regarding funding? Morgan suggested they put together a quick proposal, just in case they asked for one. They quickly came up with a budget request for the near-term of $270,000 for the 2007-2008 season. But depending on how things went, they were also planning on bringing up the need to upgrade the existing fleet of U.S. sleds, as well as the idea of building two new 2-man sleds and a new 4-man sled, which was the much-discussed "sled of the future" Bo-Dyn wanted to create for the 2010 Olympics.

When they got to USOC headquarters and were shown to the conference room, they were more than a little surprised to find that the USOC head, Jim Scherr, a NASCAR fan, was star-struck by Bodine. He was a big NASCAR fan and car buff. The Bo-Dyn Project Board was so used to having Geoff around that they barely thought of him as a celebrity. Scherr asked Bodine about his NASCAR wins and wanted to talk about his muscle car. He asked Bodine and Cuneo how he could get more horsepower out of a 1971 Plymouth Roadrunner that he owned. Shortly after the Roadrunner discussion, Scherr asked, "Why don't you give us a proposal?"

With things going so smoothly, they decided to push their advantage. As Goodwin says, "We decided that we were going to go big or go home. Morgan pulled out the planned presentation out of his brief case and handed it over the table. The Bo-Dyn Board presented their ideas for future sled construction and made the point that, presently, without a strong USBSF Board, the Bo-Dyn Project didn't want the funding to go through the interim USBSF Board. It should go straight to the Bo-Dyn Project so they could get right to the work of refurbishing sleds and building the next generation prototype sled that was sorely needed to bring the national team's performance to the next level. They suggested that Bo-Dyn could invoice the USOC and payment could be made out directly to the Bo-Dyn Project. They also brought up the idea of Bo-Dyn and the USOC agreeing to a three-year plan to develop the sled of the future, which Whelen had already been supporting.

The meeting had been fantastic. In the end, it was the entire team that contributed — Morgan's enthusiasm, Cuneo's design and engineering track record, Kurze's ability to bring in Whelen and other sponsors, the legal and business acumen of Goodwin and Vester, as well as Kurtz' knowledge of the USOC and USBSF funding platforms. But it was Bodine and his presence who sold it. "In the end, I think they believed in the team's ability to perform," Goodwin says. "But it was Geoff they really trusted." Of course, Holcomb winning the World Cup title the previous season with seven gold medals using a radical new steering design didn't hurt. When the Bo-Dyn team members left the room for their plane, they were giddy. Goodwin stated flatly to the rest of the Board: "We're getting funded; it's just a question of how much."

In a letter to John Morgan from Jay Warwick of the USOC on May 30 of 2007, the USOC formally approved the $270,000 and laid out the groundwork for future funding for sled construction. Then, in June 2007, the USOC approved a grant to support the development of bobsleds and bobsled technologies for the benefit of the United States athletes. This grant provided a portion of the funding Bo-Dyn required to develop the bobsled technologies. The meeting in Colorado Springs was essentially the birth of the Night Train because Cuneo needed the promise of funding if we were going to invest Chassis Dynamics in developing the "sled of the future." "With that USOC funding and the money that Whelen had put in, that was the funding source for the Night Train," Goodwin says. Everything seemed on track. Except that everyone was in for a big surprise.

A Scare for Holcomb – and the Bo-Dyn Project

Holcomb had been dealing for years with a secret that had slowly pulled him away from his crewmates even as they were experiencing so much success on the track. Years earlier, Holcomb had been diagnosed with Keratoconus, a degenerative eye disease that affects 1 in 1,000, and can lead to blindness without a cornea transplant.

By spring 2007, his eyesight was deteriorating to the point where it was clear that he was going blind. But a bobsled pilot who decided to get a cornea transplant "might as well hold a news conference and announce his retirement," Holcomb jokes. But that Holcomb line is closer to the truth than not. It turns out that cornea transplants need to be done one eye at a time, with a recovery period of about two years for each eye. Two cornea transplants would put Holcomb out of action long enough to eliminate the 2010 Olympics from his plans. It was seven years until the 2014 Games in Sochi. As Holcomb says, he might as well have announced his retirement if he were going to take the cornea transplant path. "The weird thing was that it was just when I was hitting my stride as a driver," Holcomb says. "It was like I was two people, one on the track and one off." From one European ski village to the next, his team would take home gold in the bright, crisp sunshine even as Holcomb's world grew darker and darker. He even worried, despite his remarkable feel and skill as a driver – "After I got the hang of it, I've never not felt in complete control driving a bobsled," he says – that he could miss something on the track because of his disease and injure his teammates in a crash.

The illness he was hiding, which Holcomb writes about in his memoir, *And Now I See*, had a very noticeable effect on his personality. "He did have a more closed personality at some point," Tomasevicz says, thinking back on those days. "But no one ever brought up the fact that he was sort of withdrawing when off the track. Steve can be an introvert, and we knew he didn't like to be confronted with anything that was going on. But we also knew he was going through some personal things."

Holcomb hit rock bottom in 2007 when he swallowed a boatload of pills chased with a good amount of Jack Daniels Tennessee Whiskey while attending a weekend sponsor event in Colorado Springs. After that incident, he knew he had to tell his coach, Brian Shimer, as well as his teammates, that he was legally blind.

The team was stunned, but the last thing on their minds was a bobsled race in the European Alps. In fact, even his eyesight was a secondary concern. Knowing Holcomb and the fact that he had fought the demons of depression before, it was their teammate's mental health that concerned them. "We didn't know what would happen next, what kind of path he was going down," Tomasevicz says. "It was very comforting to see how everyone in the program rallied around to help him in any way, including trying to find other doctors who could help him. And that had nothing to do with 'Are we going to be able to do well in 2010 at the Olympics?'"

On December 22, 2007, a doctor named Brian Boxer Wachler performed an experimental procedure on Holcomb that halted the degenerative assault Holcomb's eyesight in its tracks. The noninvasive procedure uses ultraviolet light to activate the vitamin riboflavin in the corneas. The following March, Wachler surgically implanted a lens behind the lens of each eye. Fortunately, the process turned out to be successful. Today, Holcomb's worldview has been changed because this revolutionary treatment, now known as Holcomb C3-R, was out there for years; but the medical community collectively dismissed it as too radical. Holcomb, when he has time, advocates for the procedure.

But back in the winter of 2008, Holcomb had more immediate concerns. Now that he could see again, he had to readjust and relearn everything to be able to steer. In fact, his sight was so good that the brightness of the snow, together with the sharpness of the images, was disorienting. He started not cleaning off his goggles to let a dirty film build up and take some of the edge of the incoming information that his brain now had to process.

Briglia, in fact, believes that Holcomb's eye condition, as terrible as it was for Holcomb, helped turn him into the pilot he developed into. Having to rely mostly on feel and instinct as his eyesight deteriorated, Holcomb was using every sense to find that the line down the hill, registering subtle changes in topography and the feel of the sled on the ice.

For the Bo-Dyn Project team, news of Holcomb's successful surgery put things back on track. Now they had the driver who could bring home the gold. "Honestly, no other driver could have won a gold medal other than Steve," Goodwin says. "Could Mike Kohn or John Napier have medaled with Holcomb's push athletes? Maybe. But Holcomb was the best driver in the history of U.S. Bobsledding."

Chapter Nine

The Night Train Cometh

I F THE BO-DYN Project was going to build the "sled of the future" for Vancouver, it had to work together as smoothly as a Holcomb-driven sled. Another development from the action-packed 2007 season illustrated just how well the Bo-Dyn Board could now work together.

For years, the U.S. was hampered by the fact that they didn't have a maintenance building for the sleds on Mount Van Hoevenberg, a comfortable spot where they store sleds and tools and have the room to work on the sleds. Particularly with the NASCAR approach to constant maintenance and continuous improvement that the Bo-Dyn Project had instilled, it was critical that such a structure be built.

After the second Bodine Challenge in January 2007, a company called Mesco Building Solutions, which was involved in building NASCAR garages, heard about the event and told Kurze and Geoff Bodine's brother, Todd Bodine, that they could potentially be interested in helping the project. They were subsequently invited to the 2008 Geoff Bodine Challenge. Getting such a company as a sponsor would be a great opportunity to further imprint NASCAR on USA bobsledding. For the 2008 Bodine Challenge, Mesco executives Ken Williams and Rusty Deen hitched a ride and joined the NASCAR drivers coming up for the event on the Hendrick's plane. They fell in love with bobsledding, and Mesco committed to providing a new sled garage, targeting the 2009 Bodine Challenge for completion of the project.

To christen the building in just one short year, however, everything would have to run like clockwork. The Bo-Dyn Board was now itself running like a veteran bobsled team, with everyone knowing his role and moving in the same direction with highly coordinated movements. Morgan went through Tony Carlino, a former bobsledder who was then the Lake Placid track manager, to convince the Olympic Authority to provide land for the building. To get the labor for the project, the Board used its NASCAR connections. Joe Giacin, a friend of the Bo-Dyn Project who had been hosted many times at NASCAR events by Whelen and Phil Kurze, served as head of the International Union of Operating Engineers in the Northeast U.S. Giacin gave his support to the construction of the building, and Morgan made a presentation to several union leaders at the union hall in Plattsburgh, New York, about 40 miles northeast of Lake Placid. He emphasized the Made in America theme of the Bo-Dyn Project and directly asked for help constructing the building. It also helped that a few of the union heads had connections to bobsledding either as former athletes, officials, or simply fans of the sport.

The union gave the thumbs-up, and local union heads John Donoghue and Jeff Kellogg coordinated the effort, directing a group of hardy union volunteers in November and December 2008. "Unions heavily support the idea of made in America in general," Morgan says. "It would be 20 degrees below zero, and these guys would be here working for free, freezing their butts off working like you wouldn't believe it. We got help from so many people."

On January 5, 2009 – right on schedule – the building was officially opened at the 2009 Bodine Challenge, Geoff Bodine christened the structure by smashing a champagne bottle in the company of fellow NASCAR drivers, sponsors, and media. The opening of the bobsled building also illustrated how the Bodine Challenge concept was now working to the benefit of USA Bobsled and its athletes.

But back in October 2007, the feel-good construction of the sled building was many months off. That month the USOC named Darrin Steele as the new executive director of the USBSF. Steele was a former member of the USA team and Shimer's brakeman in the 2-man competition at the 2002 Salt Lake Games, and thus very familiar with the Bo-Dyn Project. On October 28, 2007, reps of Bo-Dyn had a conference call with the members of the new USBSF Board about the Bo-Dyn-USBSF relationship, a meeting at which the Bo-Dyn Board specifically expressed concern about Bo-Dyn's intellectual property being leaked to, and used by, others to build bobsleds for the benefit of athletes in other countries. On January 8, 2008, Bo-Dyn and USBSF met at the Bodine Challenge and entered into a contract valid through the 2010 Olympic Winter Games specifying that Bo-Dyn owned the intellectual property underpinning the sleds, while the USBSF owned the sleds.

The Emergence of Justin Olsen and the 2007-2008 Season

Still another important milestone in 2007 was the emergence of the man who would become the last piece of the puzzle for the Night Train crew. Growing up in San Antonio, Justin Olsen and his younger brothers, James and John, used to love watching *Cool Runnings*, which was about as close as Olsen had ever gotten to an actual bobsled before 2007. Like Mesler and his track and field experience at the University of Florida, Olsen's introduction to bobsledding was borne out of a dashed dream. Olsen was a high school football star who was recruited by a number of schools. He was always interested in the military and jumped at the chance to attend the United States Air Force Academy, where he continued his football career. Unhappy there, Olsen decided the Air Force Academy was not for him. Back in San Antonio, casting about for what to do next, Olsen heard about NFL Combine-like test for the U.S. national bobsled team.

"When I told my family what I was doing," Olsen says, "my brothers thought that was the funniest thing they'd ever heard because their only association with bobsledding was *Cool Runnings*, so they just laughed at me."

There was nothing funny about Olsen's performance when he showed up for his first training experience in the autumn of 2007. He excelled in the push competition. And once he went down a track for real, Olsen was hooked. Ironically, Olsen always had a fear of roller coasters growing up, so on his first few runs he just hung on for dear life. "Sure it's scary at first," Olsen says. "But the skills needed matched my athleticism, so here was a sport where I could compete at the very highest level. It can be frightening, but there's also the adrenaline rush."

When the news came that he had made the World Cup team as a rookie at just 20 years old – pushing for John Napier — he knew he had made the right choice. College and his interest in engineering could wait. Olsen progressed very quickly, helping Napier to some decent showings in St. Moritz and Konigssee that winter of 2008.

Olsen was just 21 when the chance of a lifetime came the next season. He had been pushing well again in training when Pavel Jovanovic hurt himself. Olsen was elevated to the marquee sled of the entire program, the 4-man USA-1; which, of course, was Holcomb's sled. In just his second year, Olsen was joining a team that had won multiple races, multiple medals, and multiple events. Holcomb was a veteran since 1998, Tomasevicz since 2004, and Mesler since 2000. Olsen's arrival and seemingly charmed route to the USA-1 was a much different path than the rigorous one that Holcomb or Mesler had trudged up to the top of their profession on.

Besides being a phenomenal athlete, Olsen also had a bit of the class clown in him. He was able to keep things light-hearted with his easy-going smile and propensity to joke around. But Olsen, understandably given his relative youth, was also a bit more immature than his teammates. Being a great push athlete was a lot different than being on a successful team with the likes of Holcomb. "So you have all these veterans, and you have a kid who has been around for a year," Holcomb says. "I think that first year with us he didn't do a lot off the track except for hanging out and drink beer in Lake Placid. We had to be pretty tough on him and deliver the message that we weren't all there together to be friends and party. We were there to win, and that's it. We were pretty hard on him, but it worked."

It was usually Mesler who had to be the bad guy, though, and he didn't mind delivering "the message of the week" to Olsen that he had to grow up a little faster. Mesler knew what Holcomb wanted, which was to get across the message that they weren't all there to hang around bars for fun. His demeanor toward Olsen was often like that of a big brother toward a spoiled kid brother. For Mesler, the idea was to ride Olsen hard, so that when there was real pressure in the Olympics, nothing could be worse for Olsen than how Mesler treated him. "For Justin, I figured there would be no extra special pressure because he'd gotten hammered by me for three years," Mesler says.

Olsen, for his part, sometimes thought that he was being unfairly targeted, but understood the situation almost like a rite of passage. "You know, there was a lot of times when I thought I was being singled out," Olsen says. "But I also understood that I had a commitment to the team, and that was their way of saying that this was a big deal, a serious commitment, and my performance impacted them. So I realized I had to dial things back."

Holcomb now had an extremely talented trio of push athletes behind him, and it was time for him to think about his commitment, as well. When it came to his 4-man team, Holcomb wanted to be the opposite of Hays. In that way, Hays' management style was helpful in showing how *not* to run a team. Holcomb realized he didn't have to control everything. Mesler ran the push crew and rode Olsen when he needed riding. He worked on the runners when they needed working on. "I might talk to Steve and say what I thought of something," Holcomb says. "And then Steve would lead the three of them as the push athletes. We all wanted to be there; we all wanted to fight for each other. I hope the guys will look back and think that we were all for each other so that we could win together."

Like a family, everyone soon settled into their roles in the sled, but also their roles in the group dynamics. As the pilot, Holcomb was the "hero" figure, Mesler was the older brother pushing everyone, Olsen was the mascot, and Tomasevicz the one who energized everyone with his enthusiasm. The group even worked with a sports psychologist named Ken Vaughn on how to work together and get along together off the track.

Meanwhile, in March 2008, the Vancouver track had been officially approved for international use. A select group of pilots was brought in to inaugurate the track for testing. In a foreshadowing of incidents to come, Russian pilot Alexander Zubkov crashed in Turn 13, a treacherous spot that Holcomb would later name "Turn 50-50," as in the chances of getting through it. Canadian Olympic gold medalist from 1998, Pierre Lueders, also had a spectacular crash in the same spot on the very next day. After Germany's Lange barely made it down in a 4-man sled, the normally mild-mannered three-time Olympic champion told the East German engineers who had designed the track that they had made a mistake on Turn 13, that the track was too fast for the curve design and would result in many crashes in the years ahead.

The Sled of the Future

Up to this point, the Bo-Dyn Project had not been known for one sled in particular – the one machine that could serve as a metaphor for the whole endeavor. Instead, it was their NASCAR philosophy of customization that defined it. But now with funding from the USOC to supplement Whelen and other sponsors, Cuneo and company were gunning for that next generation of sleds.

To move forward, Cuneo planned to take stock of the major differences that distinguished Bo-Dyn sleds from other bobsleds, and see where improvements could be made. The first big difference between Bo-Dyn sleds and others was the steering, which had just been re-engineered, so Cuneo didn't need to touch that. The second was the ability to customize. Before Geoff Bodine pursued American-made sleds for a new generation of sliders, bobsled athletes bought a sled, probably from a competitor from another country, and either liked it or didn't. If the team didn't like it, they would have to save up and take their chance on another one or accept that they were stuck with that sled.

The third was the articulation. The Bo-Dyn team, steeped in NASCAR, had borrowed from race car design the idea of a torsion bar set at the front of the sled to control the front and back pieces of the sled. When the sled turns around a corner and then comes into a straight-away, the front should be lined up perfectly with the back piece of the sled, and something needs to facilitate that flex. When a torsion bar twists, it returns, spring-like. Its implementation allowed the Bo-Dyn team to experiment with a heavier bar or softer bar to adjust to the track. While the steering couldn't be adjusted during an event, one could make adjustments to the torsion bar to set the spring in the torsion bar more or less.

Fourth, there were the innovations to what could be called the suspension. A bobsled doesn't technically have a classic suspension system because there are no wheels for the rest of the vehicle to be attached to. But the adaptions related to the flexibility of the chassis, how the chassis is attached to the sled body, how all the parts of the sled interacted under the strain of going down the track at 80-90 miles per hour, how certain materials tended to dampen or not dampen the efficiency of the sled – all of these factors affected the smoothness of the ride. For pilots and push athletes, this had always been one of the most immediate benefits of a Bo-Dyn machine. The ride was exceptionally smooth, and the sleds made very little sound compared to other types of sleds. The one distinctive sound the sleds did have, incidentally, was a whistling sound that always befuddled the Europeans, who thought it signaled another kind of speed advantage. But it was simply caused by the front axle boot covers and the high-velocity air that was generated.

And, fifth, there were the aerodynamic advances concerning how Cuneo and company had shaped the sleds to decrease wind drag. In all five of these areas, except the steering element, anything and everything was on the table for discussion when it came to retooling the sleds. "Certain things like the smooth ride of the sled we felt like had been getting better and better every year," Cuneo says. "But for what became the Night Train, we wanted to improve everything again."

With the likelihood of an extremely fast Olympic track in Vancouver first and foremost in their minds, the design team quickly homed in on aerodynamics as an area where more than incremental changes could be made. Something that the Bo-Dyn Project team had noticed time and again in wind testing was that the lower the athletes got in the sled, the less drag there was and the faster the sled went. While that might seem obvious, the testing showed that the push athletes being down flush with the top surfaces of the sled while racing wasn't low enough. If they could be down below the imaginary plane that marked the top of the sled, it would rocket down the hill even faster.

So Cuneo and Briglia did some computer models of a sled with a lot more room in the bottom of the sled, which would allow push athletes to crouch extremely low after loading into the sled, while still maintaining comfort. Indeed, watching tapes of the Night Train in ensuing years, many times just Holcomb is visible; it doesn't look as if anyone else is even in the sled. Geoff Bodine points to this design decision as the single biggest innovation in the sled that became the Night Train. "Our biggest advantage with the Night Train was that we worked very hard to build the bottom of the sled so the athletes could get in there and get very low," Bodine says.

By October 2008, just before training for the 2008-2009 World Cup season was to begin, the sled of the future prototype was ready to be shipped to Park City, Utah, so Holcomb and the push athletes could test it. Whenever a sled is delivered for testing, it just has a primer coat on it, because if a change is needed, removing the hard coat is that much more difficult.

When the sled was taken out of the truck, Holcomb, Mesler, Tomasevicz and Olsen gathered around to examine Cuneo's new creation. Immediately the new design of the bottom of the sled was apparent as they loaded in to check it out. "The first thing I noticed was how low you could get into it," Olsen says. To Holcomb, it felt great right away. After a very fast first run, they tested it several times against their current sled. "It destroyed the sled we were using at that point," Mesler says. "I want to say it was by two-tenths of a second per run, which is big." Everyone loved it, and Cuneo was thrilled because he had secretly anticipated that the results would be spectacular. "Okay," Cuneo told the team. "I'll meet you in Europe in January; we're all set." Mesler responded: "What do you mean January in Europe? We're taking this to Lake Placid to train and then on the World Cup circuit, this December!"

Cuneo explained that, as usual practice, the sled had to go back to Connecticut to get the hard coat of paint on and for various tweaks. "No way, man," Holcomb weighed in. "We're taking this on tour." Someone on the team asked if the sled would be slower without the hard coat of paint.

"Well, of course not," Cuneo said. "Well," Mesler said. "We don't care about the paint. You can't expect us to go on tour with a sled that is two-tenths of a second slower than the one we have right here."

The racer in Cuneo really couldn't argue with that. He did, however, insist that he must take the sled back to Connecticut to do a few mechanical fixes, and then he would meet them in Lake Placid shortly after. That was enough for the team.

Back in Oxford at the Chassis Dynamics shop just a few days later, Cuneo didn't have time to put on a coat of primer and the finish. So he just left the black primer on. But something bothered him that he couldn't quite put his finger on. The sled needed……more. Cuneo, who spent his professional life in flashy NASCAR circles, thought the sled needed a little pizazz if its presentation was going to match its speed. His mind flashed to his Harley-Davidson bike that was called the "Night Train" and had a black matte finish. He went to work on a "Night Train" logo, without telling the athletes what he was up to. He didn't want them to veto his idea before he could do it justice.

Briglia drove the sled to Lake Placid a few days later. As they unloaded it, the team gathered. No one spoke at first. There was something strange about this sled. It had a big logo on it with the name "Night Train." For the uninitiated, while bobsledders sometimes have nicknames for their sleds, they don't typically plaster the name on the sled itself. It just wasn't done. According to Mesler, "We were like, 'What the hell?' No one does anything like that. And no one just had a primer coat on a sled."

And yet, as the teammates all examined it, they quickly agreed that they loved the whole package – the Night Train logo, the slightly mysterious unfinished look of the paint coating, the intimidating sparseness of the design. They couldn't help playing a practical joke on Cuneo, though, whom they knew must be anxiously awaiting their reaction to the sled, as he had gone ahead and taken the liberty of branding it for them. Mesler called Cuneo and, using his gravest voice, said, "Hey, we got the sled. And, we need to talk to you about it.'" Mesler had to hold in his laughter. "We met as a team and need to tell you something." Cuneo says he remembers thinking, "Oh my God they hate it." Mesler tortured him as long as he could and then told how awesome they all thought it looked. It was time to race – and to win.

They had the Night Train. With Holcomb, they had one of the planet's best bobsled pilots. Mesler, Tomasevicz, and Olsen were the cream of the crop regarding the push athletes. When it came to the age-old bobsled debate of spreading out the best athletes among the sleds or putting the best in one sled, the American coaches had clearly decided to put all their eggs in one basket.

And win they did. They backed up the Night Train's look with gold in Park City, silver in Innsbruck, bronze in Winterberg, and some other Top 10 finishes before Christmas.

In late January of that 2008-09 World Cup season, came the long-awaited first look at the Vancouver track. It had been a long time coming. In the world of bobsledding, it's to the home country's advantage to keep competitor training time to a minimum. That's how the Canadians were approaching their new track in Vancouver. But with the Olympics just 13 months away, Canada's Olympic Committee had to show that the Whistler Sliding Center was ready for prime time. A training week took place the last week of January to prepare for the World Cup race the weekend of February 5-7.

Cuneo's scouting report two and half years earlier had been right on the mark. The contour of the track left very little straight-away; it dropped from the start and was all big, hard turns all the way down the mountain. Designers had created what was without a doubt the world's fastest sliding track, with a 4-story drop and tight curves bound to result in heretofore unthinkable speeds for bobsleds. "We were thinking, "Oh this thing is perfect for us,'" Mesler says. As Cuneo envisioned, it was a track made for the Night Train, sort of like a serve and volleyer playing on the fast grass courts of Wimbledon. The faster the grass court, the better for a big, hard server; and the faster the track, the closer to the edge, the better for the Night Train. At no point on their training runs could Holcomb relax for even a second. To the team, it reminded them of the famously fast track at St. Moritz or, closer to home, the original track in Lake Placid – but faster than both.

The next week, the team returned to Whistler for the actual World Cup race, which was the pre-Olympic competition. There was one turn on the track that everyone knew was a real doozy. To the experienced eyes of veteran bobsledders, Turn 13 on the Whistler track was similar to a famously treacherous, hairpin turn in Altenberg, Germany, also a very difficult and fast track. Because the ice was also shaped for the luge event the week before, it was particularly tricky. After the first day of competition, there was no telling which teams would make it through unscathed. That night, the Night Train team joked how they had a 50-50 chance of making it through the turn. Holcomb wrote the new name of the turn on the back of a Chinese food takeout bag and posted it on the wall of the turn. They took some pictures and posted them on social media, and that's how Turn 13 came to be known as "50/50."

The next morning, when it was the Night Train's turn, coaches were gathered at Turn 13 as Holcomb, and his push athletes took off. The coaches were surprised when they executed a real race push, not a typical practice push like most all of the other teams. With the very fast start, they were rocketing down the track. Holcomb went through Turn 13 flawlessly, showing how he had developed, along with Germany's Lange, as one of the very top drivers in the world. Later that week Holcomb and his Night Train teammates took silver in the pre-Olympic competition, missing gold by .02 seconds. Lange, who had complained the previous year about the danger of the Whistler track, almost crashed at the 50-50 curve in the first heat and didn't compete in heat 2.

In the women's test race that same week, Americans Shauna Rohbock and her partner, Elena Meyers, won gold; Erin Pak and Michelle Rzepka won bronze, and Bree Schaaf and Emily Azevedo finished 6th, putting three USA/Bo-Dyn sleds in the top six. In fact, U.S. sleds were doing so well at the Whistler Sliding Center that at one point one of the Canadian athletes wondered aloud to Cuneo– only half-jokingly – why the Canadian Federation had built a track perfect for Bo-Dyn sleds.

In Europe that winter, rumors abounded about the new Night Train sled. Since no one thought that Bo-Dyn, which had the reputation of turning out polished, great-looking sleds, would adorn a new, marquee sled with a simple layer of primer, word around the circuit was that Cuneo and Briglia had come up with some special high-tech paint job to cut down on drag, or some other such theory. Because the thinking went, why would they leave it unfinished like that? Just as the mysterious whistling sound of the sleds gave the Europeans something to think about, so too did the urban legends circulating about the paint job.

The intimidation factor was real. It didn't hurt, of course, that the team boasted the fastest push crew and one of the best drivers in the world. Indeed, Holcomb was at the height of his driving ability in 2009. It's hard to describe the intangibles that made him better. It wasn't active steering of the sled because as those who know the sport understand when you're steering, you're slowing the sled down. The pilot wants to let the sled "run," but also needs to make sure it's at the right point on the track where it's not going to crash as it goes into and comes out of turns. It's sort of like a pitcher that's aiming the pitch as opposed to seeing home plate and just firing away. Holcomb was taking one look at the plate and firing away.

For Briglia, who had been traveling in Europe with the U.S. national team for more than 10 World Cup seasons, it was an amazing experience to think you could win every time against the world's best. "You know, if anything, I'm even more competitive than Holcomb," Briglia says. "I wanted to win every race that season. Everyone would tell me that we can't win every race, but I mean everything was clicking at that point."

The next week the World Cup circuit visited Holcomb's home town of Park City, and the Night Train won another gold medal. Then it was on to Lake Placid for the 2009 World Championships and the heavily favored Night Train did not disappoint. After four heats, Holcomb and his teammates were nearly a cumulative full second ahead of the 2nd-place team, with a winning margin of .97 seconds. They took home the World Championship for the U.S. for the first time in 50 years. Rumors were spreading like wildfire on Mount Van Hoevenberg that various national federations were offering up to $1 million on the spot for a U.S. sled, but no one on the Bo-Dyn team ever received such an offer — nor would they have entertained one. In fact, according to Cuneo, for years representatives of the various national bobsledding federations had informally come to him and other Bo-Dyn Project members, quietly asking about purchasing sleds. For example, at the FIBT annual summer congress that was staged in London in 2008, the Russian team approached Cuneo and Morgan with a blank check. "One of the reasons that no one ever came to us directly and made a formal offer with a set price for a sled was that they had felt us out for years about it, and they knew we were not entertaining any offers, we only built sleds for USA Athletes," Cuneo says.

The margin of victory at the World Championships was almost unheard of, and it was time to celebrate. After Briglia had cleaned the runners, put away the sleds in the new Bo-Dyn garage, and locked the garage up, he went into downtown Lake Placid, where things were quite rowdy. Together at the Zig Zag bar – the most popular watering hole in town for the bobsled set — was Holcomb and Lange, the defending Olympic champion. Lange, despite his rivalry with

Holcomb, was popular on the circuit and great with the crowds, knowing to smile and flash thumbs-ups signs to spectators. Much to Briglia's surprise, Lange was wearing a Night Train hat. "Andre, what are you doing with that hat?" Briglia asked him. "Well," Lange said, "After what happened this week, tonight I am a big Night Train fan."

As the Night Train and Holcomb became the talk of the bobsled world, Hays could not stay away; his competitive juices were still flowing. Retired since the 2006 Torino Olympics, Hays announced in February 2009 that he was coming back that fall for the 2009-2010 season.

Whatever success is achieved in Olympic sports on the playing field, in the gym or on the ice, the crushing economics of niche Olympic sports is always a factor. Unsurprisingly, the Night Train success hadn't resulted in much for Holcomb and the others regarding monetary reward. Holcomb would still on occasion refer to himself only half-jokingly as a "glorified volunteer." The only way Holcomb was able to stay in the sport since the late 1990s had been to live at the Olympic Training Center. That means he didn't own a house, didn't have money to invest, and didn't have anything saved for his future. That's why, when the opportunity came along to hire an agent, Holcomb jumped at it. Brant Feldman became

Holcomb's agent 45 days after the World Championships in Lake Placid. At the time, Holcomb was $43,000 in debt. Feldman's job was to monetize Holcomb's achievements, to "get this kid out of the hole."

Once Feldman took over, Holcomb did land a few long-term endorsements, such as a contract with Under Armour. The deals were such that he would say he gets bonuses when he medaled on the World Cup Circuit and in the Olympics; he could also get bonuses if he could get the Under Armour logo in the media. With those bonuses, Holcomb could elevate his salary by $40,000 or $50,000 per year, which would be doubling his salary. And Holcomb was one of the lucky ones.

The business end of things was also a concern for the Bo-Dyn Board during the 2009 off-season. In May 2009, Darrin Steele of the USBSF Board and Hays, out of retirement and making mischief once again, visited Bo-Dyn's technical partner, Exa Corporation – a wind tunnel technology company — without anyone on the Bo-Dyn team knowing. The Bo-Dyn Board considered Steele and Hays' visit to Exa to be a severe breach of trust by Steele and the USBSF. Exa was a longtime partner of Bo-Dyn's that provided a significant amount of service and possessed a huge trove of Bo-Dyn's proprietary knowledge relating to the research and design of the Bo-Dyn bobsleds. Brad Duncan, head of Exa's land vehicle aerodynamic division and his father, Lewis, had worked with Bodine and Cuneo during Bodine's NASCAR days and played an important role in the early days when wind testing was such an important tool for the initial Cuneo designs.

While the Bo-Dyn team regarded Exa as a highly professional organization that presumably knew that it shouldn't share any proprietary Bo-Dyn information with a completing sled builder, the Bo-Dyn Board, understandably, was concerned that the USBSF was disclosing Bo-Dyn's intellectual property to Hays in violation of the contract they had signed.

In June 2009, Bo-Dyn representatives again met with the USBSF Board of Directors and, among other things, reiterated Bo-Dyn's concerns about the protection of its intellectual property. The Bo-Dyn Project Board wanted to make sure their interests were protected because there was a potentially historic season coming up. The Night Train would be gunning for gold in Vancouver.

Chapter Ten

Just Another Race

GOING INTO THE 2009-2010 World Cup season, few could remember the last time that a European bobsled power such as Germany or Switzerland wasn't the World Cup or Olympic favorite. As the team to beat, the Night Train Team squad had a huge target on its back.

But that didn't mean the Bo-Dyn Project team was resting on its laurels. In the summer of 2009, Cuneo was experimenting with some designs for a new 2-man chassis. He settled on a design he thought would be effective in Vancouver, but couldn't convince any of the top drivers – Holcomb, John Napier, or Rohbock on the women's side – to use them. While Cuneo was disappointed, he knew enough about racing equipment to bide his time; his new sleds might eventually see race-day competition – one never knows.

It was clear in the very first race of the year in Holcomb's hometown of Park City. The local press made a big show of the prodigal son returning, even if Holcomb's career was much more intertwined with Lake Placid than Park City. The first two heats took place in a raging blizzard, and a Canadian, Lyndon Rush, won the race, with Holcomb driving the Night Train to a 7th place finish. The Canadian team celebrated as if it had already won the World Cup points race. "In the middle of a snowstorm like that, every sled was all over the place," Olsen said. "It was almost a throwaway race." Hays, in his first official World Cup event in more than three years, medaled in the 2-man, serving notice that his comeback was indeed serious.

But it was already evident in Park City that the Night Train and its effect on the sport – not Hays — would be the topic at the center of the bobsledding universe until the Vancouver Olympics. For example, during the off-season, the back half of Germany's sleds seemed to have been retooled to match the design of the Night Train. As soon as they took a look at the German sleds, Olsen and Mesler remembered that they had watched German team assistants taking dozens of pictures of the Night Train during the World Championships in Lake Placid in 2009. What mattered, of course, was how the German sled performed on the track.

The next stop was Holcomb's adopted hometown of Lake Placid, where just a few months earlier Holcomb and the crew had dethroned Andre Lange and his team as 4-man world champions. The *Colbert Report* host Stephen Colbert did a feature on the Night Train during the training days leading up to the competition in Lake Placid. As part of the segment, Colbert took Mesler's place in the sled for a fun run from halfway down the track. After they crossed the finish line, Colbert got out, announced that he was happy to be going to Vancouver to compete for America, and then yelled out so the crowd of spectators could hear: "Where's Mesler? Who is going to tell him that I'm taking his place?"

The Night Train Effect

Joking aside, though, USA-1 went on to win gold in Lake Placid and followed that with gold in Cesana, gold in Winterberg, silver in Altenberg, silver in Konigssee, and a 4th-place finish in St. Moritz. The winning created even more attention around the sled, which in turn played into the mythology surrounding the Night Train that winning was inevitable. The athletes were never "jealous" of the sled's attention because they knew that other teams were already half-beaten at the top of the track. A friend of Mesler's printed up a load of black Night Train t-shirts for the team to hand out, jet black tops with a yellow "Night Train" blazed across the front. "The sled became us, and we became the sled," Mesler says. Meanwhile, Hays, who had qualified for the Vancouver Games along with Holcomb and Napier, crashed a Latvian-made 4-man sled that he was piloting for the very first time while on a training run in Winterberg, suffering a concussion that would end his career.

Mesler explains why the psychology behind the Night Train sled being unbeatable was so helpful to their efforts. "The German, the Swiss, the Russians, they could go and train harder to get a better start," Mesler says. "Or maybe they could study Holcomb and his lines down the mountain, and they can improve there. But if our sled is just a lot better than theirs, they're screwed. They have no chance."

The truth, though, is that while the sled was critical, the foursome of Holcomb, Mesler, Tomasevicz, and Olsen had used the 2009 summer off-season to make sure that they came into this Olympic year at their very best. Their hunger to cap their success with the gold medal that would break the 62-year U.S men's winless streak was palpable to the coaches and other athletes. Between July 2009 and the Vancouver Games in February 2010, there were only three days in which some combination of the Night Train team were not together training, working out, or traveling. One of them was Christmas Day 2009 when they all decided they were sick of each other and went their separate ways.

And, as much as the Night Train sled helped create a psychological advantage for the team, the foursome still had their own mental demons to fight. Holcomb was continuing to work with a sports psychologist, partly to deal with his anxiety that one wrong move by him at the helm of the Night Train could ruin the team's 4-man Olympic chances. The paradox, of course, is that you have to *treat* the Olympics like a normal race. Coming in thinking you have to do something special is the kiss of death because you won't perform as you normally do. "You develop certain rituals," Holcomb says. "If you start to treat the Olympic Games as something different and don't stick to those rituals, you are going to perform in a way that's different and not in a relaxed manner." The idea, Holcomb kept telling himself, was to think of the Olympic race as just another day, just another race, just another heat. "When you start thinking, 'Oh my God, I'm at the Olympics, don't' mess this up,' that's when people panic and mess up."

The Arch Rival

Throughout the 2009-2010 season, Team Holcomb had been getting the better of Germany-1, driven by Lange. Early on in the World Cup 4-man points race, they were well ahead of Lange's team. Still, at the Vancouver Games, Lange would be going for his third straight 4-man Olympic medal, a feat that had never been achieved. Overall, the Germans were going for their fifth straight Olympic gold in the 4-man. They – and Lange — were the kings of the hill until somebody knocked them off.

Indeed, going into Vancouver, Lange was already one of the most decorated pilots in bobsled history. In addition to his two 4-man gold medals, he had also taken the gold in the 2006 2-man. Lange also had four 4-man world championships, one 2-man world championship, and four combined world championships to his credit. Between his 2-man and 4-man sleds, he took home an astounding 14 different medals at the year-ending FIBT World Championships, including 8 gold medals.

Lange's physical size was also intimidating. He looked the part of the untouchable, unbeatable champion in a sport in which the U.S. was perennially behind the eight ball. Lange was a former luger and, according to Frank Briglia, lugers often develop an excellent feel for the ice at any particular track and how that surface will affect a sled's movement. That sixth sense can help produce a fine bobsled pilot.

But Lange was also a different breed than many of his German predecessors, who tended to be aloof when interacting with bobsled athletes from other countries. And why not? They were used to the pampering that came with big budgets from the FES; for decades they had had the best equipment, and their athletes were always second to none. They wore their disdain for other countries on their sleeves — as an intimidation element, certainly, but also because they truly felt that way.

Lange, though, was different from his German predecessors. Much looser, more humble, and far more willing to just be a regular guy — much as he was in Lake Placid after the 2009 World Championship, sharing a beer with Holcomb – Lange totally reset the dynamic between the German team and its competitors. "Andre changed the way that the German team raced," Cuneo says. "Until he came along, they didn't interact with other countries much. But when Andre was at the very peak of his career – between 2004 and 2008 – he was just the nicest guy."

One of his favorite things to do with Cuneo was just walk up and pick him off the ground. When mobile phones became ubiquitous on the circuit, Lange loved taking selfies with the other athletes and even the fans. Because of the tone Lange set, the deep freeze that had defined the whole German bobsledding team started to thaw. Soon enough, the German coaches and the pilots of the other German sleds became more approachable as well.

For Cuneo, the best of times was the period between 2006 and 2010, when a fierce rivalry emerged between Holcomb and Lange, but also between the FES and the Bo-Dyn Project – and yet, it was a rivalry based on mutual respect. "There was this tension," Cuneo says. "Both groups were so far ahead of the other countries that it was ridiculous. So we were pushing each other. It was a lot of fun." That sense of respect was evident as, after every race he attended, Lange would approach Cuneo and shake his hand.

The Americans get credit for fostering the detente, as well. Briglia's propensity to assist other teams with delicate tweaks of their sleds, Holcomb's willingness to use his computer geekdom to help others troubleshoot their devices, and the overall sense of fair play that the Bo-Dyn engineers and mechanics projected were all positive forces in the sport.

The ethos Cuneo brought to racing, for example, is illustrated by this anecdote told by Michael Nitsch, Germany's top sled designer for years. At one event, Cuneo was acting as one of the inspectors who confirm before every World Cup race that teams are not cutting corners with the equipment. He spotted an irregularity in the sled of a top German team; there was a problem with the symmetry of the axle. As it turned out, the axle part wasn't approved by the German Bobsled Federation; it was a similar part made by a different manufacturer and not allowed in competition. But instead of raising a red flag and characterizing the irregularity as cheating, Cuneo recognized the oversight for what is was, accepted Nitsch's explanation, and then helped the Germans install a regulation part in time for the competition. This was part of the NASCAR attitude, as well. Race as hard as hell against your opponent, but be fair-minded and magnanimous off the track. "What would you call it? Maybe integrity," Nitsch says. "It was clear to us that Cuneo never wanted to disqualify people, win or lose on the track."

As for the personal rivalry between Holcomb and Lange, the mutual respect hadn't translated to a real friendship, mostly because the language barrier hadn't let them connect. Mesler, on the other hand, learned to speak some German through the years, and because of that, communicated a little more with Lange, whom he liked very much. Personal rivalries in bobsledding, after all, are secondary to the challenge of the mountain, not to mention the challenge of not beating yourself. "Realistically, I'm racing myself, not Andre," is how Holcomb puts it. "He has no absolutely no effect on what I do. He's not throwing snowballs at me as I go down the hill, trying to distract me."

Away from the World Cup rivalry with the Germans, life went on for the Bo-Dyn Project. In January 2010, the fifth Bodine Challenge, sponsored by Lucas Oil, was held. The night before the race, Morgan and his fellow organizers brought the drivers to the Olympic Center for a reception where the Team USA's Miracle on Ice hockey win occurred over the USSR in 1980. The race car drivers like Joey Logano, Jeg Coughlin, Morgan Lucas, Boris Said and others were at center ice taking pictures when, all of a sudden, the lights wet dim and down from the rafters came USA Hockey jerseys with the names of the race car drivers stitched on the back. Playing in the background was Al Michaels' famous call, "Do you believe in Miracles?" A nice touch, yes, but Olympic hockey gold from a quarter-century earlier wasn't really the gold medal that the Bo-Dyn Project was most interested in.

Gold in Vancouver was what everyone who'd ever had anything to do with the Bo-Dyn Project had in mind.

Qualifying for the Games and Getting into the Olympic Mindset

When Hays suffered his concussion in December, it opened the door for another American sled at the Vancouver Games. Holcomb and fellow U.S. pilot, John Napier, were sure to qualify over the World Cup Season. As one of the top three nations in the World Cup standings, the U.S. would be eligible to field three 4-man teams. On the same weekend that Hays was injured, Mike Kohn – a 37-year-old pilot who had won a bronze medal pushing for Brian Shimer's 4-man sled eight years earlier in Salt Lake City, and whom Dan Goodwin had helped fund all those years before – was racing in what he assumed would be the last race of his career, an Americas Cup race in Lake Placid. The Americas Cup is the "B" tour, the North American version of the larger and far more important World Cup circuit. But with another opening for a U.S. sled available because of the Hays' injury, Kohn could make the World Cup team and go to Europe to try to gather enough World Cup points to go to Vancouver. The rub was that he had to finish first or second in the Americas Cup race in Lake Placid in December 2009.

Kohn crashed a 4-man sled on the final day of training and, with just an hour left of available training time, everyone on the mountain that day assumed his quest had ended; after all, his sled was totaled. But Kohn hustled over to the Whelen Bo-Dyn garage, pulled out an old Bo-Dyn 4-man sled, threw some runners on it, and jumped in with his crew for a training run. Remarkably, Kohn drove that 4-man sled to victory in the qualifying race the next day. The garage, the extra sled, the fact that the sled was maintained and ready to go – these were all examples of how the Bo-Dyn Project changed American bobsledding. "Not only is there rarely a backup sled available for a "B" level race – which the Americas Cup is – but to have it just sitting there a couple of hundred yards away in the Bo-Dyn garage, pretty much ready to go, that's incredible," Morgan says. "And then he won with it." Having made the World Cup team, Kohn went on to Europe after Christmas, where a top ten finish in St. Moritz qualified his 4-man sled for the Vancouver Games.

Before announcing the final 4-man teams, USBSF CEO, Darrin Steele, had considered shuffling the deck for the 4-man. With so many strong push athletes, to him, it wasn't a given that everyone who pushed together should stay together. By spreading the strongest push athletes throughout the three teams, the U.S. could conceivably bring to Vancouver three sleds that could potentially medal. But in the end, the idea of breaking up Team Holcomb carried too much risk. "If you think about where the teams were ranked, Holcomb number one, Napier second, and Kohn sixth, that's a pretty strong case to go with the teams that pushed together," Steele told the press at the time. What the reaction from Holcomb and his teammates – not to mention Cuneo, Briglia, and Bodine – would have been if Team Holcomb had been broken up for the Olympics is anyone's guess. It likely wouldn't have been pretty. As for the 2-man, as is generally the case in World Cup races, the U.S. Olympic teams in Vancouver were made up of a driver of a 4-man sled paired with one of his push athletes: Holcomb with Tomasevicz, Napier with brakeman Langton, and Kohn with Nick Cunningham.

At the same race in St. Moritz where Kohn qualified, Lange continued a late-season resurgence, winning the 4-man for his third straight 4-man World Cup victory. Lange, clearly, was adept at peaking just in time for the Games. The Germans also had qualified three sleds for the Games, which would lend a strong German-U.S. flavor to the 4-man.

About the time that Kohn was qualifying for the Games, an old acquaintance of Holcomb's made headlines by bringing up a topic that Holcomb, too, had been thinking a lot about. Bode Miller, one of the greatest ski racers of all time, had been injured for much of the 2009-2010 World Cup ski race circuit after getting hurt in a friendly volleyball game. Given his lack of training, Miller said that he wasn't that focused on the Olympics anyway, because they just came along once every four years, and here he was winning multiple World Cup races every year and dominating his circuit. Miller went on to point out how the Olympics didn't do a good job of identifying the best racers in the world, but rather who got "hot" for two days in February once every four years. In Torino, for example, Miller failed to win a medal at all. Conversely, many athletes who never experienced consistent success might have an unbelievable race or two at the Olympics, and their name lives on forever. U.S. skier Tommy Moe, for example, took home gold in the downhill and silver in the super-G in 1994 at Lillehammer, yet won only one World Cup gold medal his entire 12-year career on the U.S. national team. Talk about peaking on the right day. Or getting lucky on the right day.

Miller, being the superstar and celebrity that he was, was someone American winter athletes paid attention to. "I remember when Bode said that about the Olympics not being his focus," Mesler says. "And to be honest, it's a cop-out. Okay, maybe it's a little bit different for a skier, but the only shot for most winter Olympians to do Letterman or be on the cover of *Sports Illustrated* is to win a gold medal at the Olympics. I empathize with Bode's mindset, but I still think it's a cop-out. The gold is what matters to an Olympic athlete."

Holcomb, as a competitive junior ski racer, used to compete against Miller on the junior ski circuit. As the one ultimately held responsible for the performance of Team Holcomb, he remembers being more sympathetic than Mesler was to Miller's point. The number of variables that can prevent an athlete or a team from peaking at the Olympics is something Holcomb has broken down by the numbers, which is just the way Holcomb's thinking is wired. A driver lucky enough to pilot both a 4-man and 2-man sled for four full years will have about 64 races between Olympic Games. "This is a full-time job for 1400 days between Olympic Games," he says. "And then when days 1399 and 1400 come around, when those 65th and 66th races come around, we call it 'the Olympics.' And you somehow have to peak on those days. But that is the reality in our sport. Everyone is paying attention just once every four years."

The problem is that a team can't just focus on that goal and shoot for the Olympics. Why? Because without winning a good number of those other 64 races, a team will likely never get competitive enough and tough enough to even qualify for the Olympics. "You have to be competitive in the other years, or you'll never make it to the races called the Olympics," Holcomb says. "It's not a matter of peaking for the Olympics; we peak for every year."

Mesler, for one, was doing everything he could to get the foursome to mentally peak at Vancouver, especially given that Lange's 4-man sled seemed to be getting sharper and sharper as the season went on. Mesler wanted things to be different than in 2006. He felt that the Hays team that he pushed for in Torino didn't believe that they could beat the top European teams at the Olympics. At a press conference before the Vancouver Games, Mesler did his best Joe Namath impersonation, when the legendary New York Jets quarterback predicted a win over the favored Colts in Super Bowl III in 1969. Mesler told the accumulated throng of international press that if "we push well and Holcomb drives well – if we just do our jobs – we'll win the Olympics."

Tomasevicz kicked Mesler under the table, and his other teammates stared at the veteran, unbelieving that he would give other teams such motivating locker room material. But Mesler had a plan. "I wanted these guys to flip the switch in their heads and start thinking that *we* were the team to beat," Mesler says. "In 2006, how we showed up with a deficit mindset, like, 'I'm still not fast enough.' I didn't want us to show up with that mindset."

One man was particularly supportive of Mesler's approach of projecting confidence going into the Games. Given the success Holcomb had been having since the spring of 2007, Briglia was certain of some kind of 4-man medal. He also thought Holcomb had a shot in the 2-man with Tomasevicz as the brakeman even though Russia, Germany, and Canada, in particular, had very strong teams. Another part of Briglia's reasoning was that the U.S. had done well in the events that had been held to date at the Whistler Siding Center. "To me, I thought they had the whole package, and they just had to go take it," Briglia says. "And our track record in Vancouver was pretty strong up 'till then."

At the Olympics, the previous four years would be distilled into four heats over two days. The World Cup wins that the Night Train team had been stocking up on for two years? Well, that was fantastic. Winning the World Championships in Lake Placid for the first 4-man World Championships in five decades – extra special. But peaking at the Olympics? "That's our job," Holcomb says. "The Bo-Dyn Project started up because of what Geoff Bodine saw at the Olympics in Albertville. It wasn't some World Cup Race in Italy that got Bodine upset; it was our performance at the Olympics." Despite all of the success and 18 years of innovation under the Bo-Dyn Project umbrella, anything other than gold in Vancouver would be a disappointment.

At the Vancouver Games

The team was staying at USA House, which was a short shuttle ride away from the Whistler Sliding Center. Just hours before the Opening Ceremony, the danger of their chosen profession came into stark relief in the most tragic of ways. Georgian luger, Nodar Kumaritashvili, was killed when he lost control of his sled and was ejected from the track, slamming into a supporting beam. He died instantly. Luge may be the "purest" form of sledding as a competitive sport. The athlete (or athletes for the 2-person competition) lies on his or her back, face up and feet first. Steering is done with the legs and shoulders—much like one would remember doing as a kid— but, of course, children's sleds don't have runners. On a luge sled, the athlete exerts pressure on the runners with his or her calves; so when it comes to protection, lugers probably have even less protection than bobsledders.

However, there is one major similarity between bobsledders and lugers. Each uses the same track, with lugers typically starting from further down. The death of Kumaritashvili, then, was a frightening harbinger for everyone who would be whizzing down the track at the Whistler Sliding Center. Given the track's brief history of crashes since its inception, many of the world's sliding athletes showed up literally frightened for their lives. In fact, in the years following the Vancouver Games, track design changed significantly with uphill segments added to the course to provide a check to the speed that sliding athletes could attain.

But in Vancouver, the speed of the Vancouver track now became *the* story for the sliding sports, with Morgan being the expert being interviewed by international media about how dangerous the track was compared to other Olympic courses. Officials moved the luge start slightly lower down the mountain to decrease the maximum speed that could likely be reached.

At the Opening Ceremonies Holcomb says "they had a great time like everyone," but at this Games, Team Holcomb was all business. For Mesler, this was his third Olympics, and Holcomb and Tomasevicz were on their second (not counting Holcomb's stint as a Salt Lake City forerunner). At other Games, each had gone to watch other events, but this time there would be a minimum of hockey game viewing or shuttle bus trips to watch Miller on the ski slopes.

Even before they started the formal training week, Team Holcomb stayed within their little bobsled bubble. Particularly with the perceived danger of the track – which started at 3,044 feet above sea level before dropping 472 vertical feet — there was anxiety among the bobsled community. Tomasevicz remembered how in Torino, he just soaked everything in — wearing the Team USA logo, socializing with athletes from different countries in the international lounge in the athlete's village, trying different national culinary specialties with fellow push athletes Lorenzo Smith and Bill Schuffenhauer, and attending hockey games and downhill ski races. "Lorenzo Smith and Bill Schuffenhauer were pretty relaxed, and that rubs off," Curt says.

On the opening day of the 2-man training, the track struck quickly. Swiss pilot Beat Hefti, one of the gold medal favorites in the 2-man, sustained a concussion in a training run crash and withdrew from the competition. The Swiss were driving brand-new Citius sleds made by a consortium of Swiss companies. This was another example of a sled project that was rushed into competition and failed. A few years later, the Citius sleds would be as competitive as any on the hill, but in Whistler in 2010, they still needed more testing. Hefti's fellow Swiss pilot, Daniel Schmid, who drove Switzerland's third 2-man sled, crashed twice that day and promptly withdrew from both the 2- and 4-man competitions. When it came time to actually race, Germany dominated, with Lange winning another gold medal. Lange, incredibly, now had his fourth Olympic gold medal. Lange was obviously in top form and would be waiting for the USA in the 4-man and was now arguably the favorite. Holcomb and Tomasevicz finished in the middle of the pack of the 2-man. They had a good run going in the first run, with the third best time, before nearly crashing in the 50/50 curve. Neither of the U.S. 2-man sleds earned a medal.

During training for the 4-man race, withdrawals due to the danger of the track continued as both men's and women's teams continued to crash. The Australian 4-man entry, for example, withdrew when two of its 4-man crew suffered concussions. The head of the Australian contingent said that while they didn't make such a decision lightly, the safety of its team was paramount. Pilot Edwin Val Calker of the Netherlands, whose brother Arnold was one of his push athletes, also pulled out of the 4-man competition during training, acceding to the pleadings of Arnold's wife, who was back home reading about all the crashes on the fastest track in the world. "It didn't matter who you were," Morgan says. "The best in the world were crashing. In other Olympics, there is no real fear you are going to crash. Going into Vancouver, it had been 30 years, in Lake Placid, since drivers were afraid they were going to crash. In Vancouver, anyone could crash." There were other withdrawals unrelated to the perceived danger of the track; for example, the top Latvian 4-man team, driven by Janins Minins, had to withdraw because Minins was struck with appendicitis just before the opening ceremony. He had won the Pre-Olympic test the year before, beating Holcomb by two-hundredths of a second.

On February 22, the 11 team captains met with officials from the International Bobsled and Skeleton Federation (IBSF) to discuss potential adjustments to the track. Training runs were suspended until they came up with a solution. The main issue, not surprisingly, was the speed being generated into Turn 13 and how difficult the "50-50" turn was to negotiate. During the meeting, it was decided to slightly change the shape of Turn 11 so drivers could get high enough to more easily maneuver through Turn 12 and, after that, Turn 13. The hope was that with that decision, the track would be significantly slowed.

On Tuesday, February 23, and Wednesday, February 24, the women's competition was held. The 2009 World champion, Nicola Minichiello from Great Britain, crashed; as did German driver, Cathleen Martini, whose spectacular crash in the fourth and final was one of the very few crashes in her entire 11-year career. With their home track advantage, two Canadian teams came out on top, which was not really a surprise. What was a surprise, however, was that Erin Pac of the U.S. took bronze with her push athlete, Elana Meyers. Pac had been having a rough year, with very few good World Cup finishes to speak of. Cuneo had taken Pac, a former track athlete at Springfield College who was eager to learn more about the dynamics of bobsledding, under his wing several years before after Pac had failed to make the 2006 Olympic team. A few weeks before the 2010 Olympic trials, with her season's results not to her liking, Pac went out for coffee and pie with Cuneo – a ritual they had – where she confided in Cuneo about a loss of confidence in her abilities; and as a result, she felt she couldn't get good times with her sled.

Cuneo, as he did for most things when it came to racing, had an answer. "I told her she had nothing to lose, so why doesn't she try the sled I designed with the new chassis," Cuneo says. Pac agreed that she had nothing to lose. And she had enormous respect for Cuneo. "I decided to take a huge risk," Pac says. "I trusted Bob and finally said, 'At this point, I'll try anything.'"

Just ten days before the team was slated to leave for the Games, Pac tested the sled in Park City. The first time down she deemed it the smoothest and fastest ride she'd ever piloted. After two days of testing, Pac had a new sled, one that carried her to her bronze medal finish. Before her final run, the two sleds before her both crashed. "Whatever people say about the Whistler track is true," Pac says. "It was terrifying. But my teammate and I trusted each other, and it worked out."

The other two women's USA sleds, driven by Bree Schaaf and Shauna Rohbock, finished 5th and 6[th,] putting three Bo-Dyn sleds in the top six. It was the third straight Olympic

Games that the USA women's bobsled medaled in Bo-Dyn sleds.

The 4-man comes at the close of the Olympics, the final Friday and Saturday before the Sunday closing ceremonies. The tough part is the wait; the good part is that it's an event that everyone remembers because it's so late in the Games. But watching friends from other sports, including the other sliding sports, get their medals was hard for Team Holcomb. Not to mention that those athletes were then free to attend events and hang out until all hours, while the Night Train team had committed to being focused on gold the entire two weeks. At the Games, they are typically some sponsor parties to attend if an athlete doesn't have to train or compete. On a Tuesday, it might be a *Sports Illustrated* party, on a Wednesday maybe a Budweiser-sponsored event. For Holcomb, Mesler, Tomasevicz and Olsen, the wildest it got was maybe a little Rock Band video game competition in the arcade at USA House. "For us, a Tuesday night was just a Tuesday night and a Wednesday night was just a Wednesday night," Mesler says. "We weren't going out to all of these cocktail parties and events. We had friends in other sports who won their medals at the beginning of the Olympics and got to party like rock stars for two weeks. You could say that we were a little jealous of them."

During training, Team Holcomb grew accustomed to the trip to Blackcomb Mountain. Each remembered during the bus rides their dreams of sports stardom as kids, maybe involving the Olympics, like Holcomb and Tomasevicz, or NFL stardom, like Olsen. And here they were, maybe not exactly as they planned or envisioned it, on the cusp of Olympic glory. Holcomb remembers, for some reason, thinking back to his mother's classroom where she taught grade school, playing computer games as she graded papers, being excited to go outside to play whatever sport was in season. "Not many people can say they are the best in the whole world at what they do, and this was going to be our chance," Holcomb says.

On the last night of training, it was extremely cold, and the track was astoundingly fast, with the Night Train hitting 155 kilometers an hour, or about 95 miles per hour. "It ended up being so goddamn fast that they didn't even end up grooming the ice for the race; it would have been way too fast for the 4-man sleds," Briglia says. "The sled was really moving that last night."

As the 4-man began, heavy snow was falling, always a challenge for sliding sports. Holcomb was the first pilot down the track, due to the Night Train's number one World Cup ranking that made the team the top seed. Holcomb and the Night Train promptly set a new track record at 50.89 seconds, although Holcomb had a nervy millisecond on the 50/50 turn, losing control slightly. Of course, even when a sled sets a track record, if it goes off first in a race, one still doesn't know for sure how good the time is. Perhaps conditions are perfect, and everyone else will follow with track records of their own. The next sled down – because of his 2nd-place finish in the season-long World Cup points race — was the German sled piloted by Lange. When he crossed the finish line, and the results showed that it was .25 seconds behind, the German coaches were visibly shocked, shaking their heads in frustration and kicking at the snow. They thought there was no way that one of their top pilots of all time could be behind by that much. "We had a tremendous first heat," Mesler says. In fact, after that first run, the Night Train team was already ahead by more than the total winning margin during the last two Olympics 4-man competitions.

      The second run went even better. They came in at 50.86 for a two-heat total time of 141.75, which built, in normal circumstances, a virtually insurmountable .44 seconds lead for the Night Train over Team Lange. Speaking of Lange, he and his team were having unbelievable starts, setting new records for the start sequence in both heats. But the Night Train set a new Olympic record for the full course run, as it twice overcame the Germans' great starts. Was it Holcomb's driving that made the difference, even though Lange was no slouch himself as a pilot? Holcomb's skill at the bottom of the track was one factor, but another was what is referred to as the U.S. sled's "start velocity," which is different than the start time.

Even though Lange and his push athletes were slightly ahead after the 50 meter start time, the Night Train was going faster at the end of the start sequence at the 100-meter mark when all the riders were loaded in. In fact, the Night Train's start velocity was about .5 kilometers faster than any other sled after the first curve at the 100-meter mark. So, while the Night Train may have been a hundredth or two-hundredths of a second behind after the start, they had already made up the time about 50 meters into the race and were ahead about 200 meters in. "They had a great jump on us right at the beginning of the start," Mesler says. "But we pushed hard the whole start sequence, so by the time we were in the sled, we were right on them." The real secret was that the Night Train was designed as a more comfortable sled to enter and settle into before the first corner. Combine that with the velocity of the Night Train start, and the result was the best speed out of curve 1.

Even with their sizeable lead after two heats, no one relaxed. All it takes is one pulled hamstring, a missed step, a ruptured calf, and there goes the first U.S. men's bobsled gold medal in 62 years. Also, with the high probability of crashes, no one could celebrate – no matter how big a lead – until the competition was complete. Russia's Alexander Zubkov, who had won bronze in the 2-man race, and Wolfgang Stamfler both crashed during the first day of competition. For the Bo-Dyn Board members, it was doubly hard because the athletes were tucked away at the USA House, and there wasn't a lot of access to them during the Games except for watching them at the Whistler Sliding Center. So Cuneo, Briglia, Bodine, and the others had to stew on their own. At least Morgan was able to concentrate on his broadcasting work.

Holcomb likes to share an amusing story of the team's mindset at this point. The morning of that first day of competition, on the shuttle bus to Blackcomb, Holcomb and Mesler were gravely discussing how Lange was in "the zone," and how tough the race was going to be. "You know, it's going to be a dogfight," Mesler said to Holcomb. "This is not going to be like the World Championships last year. We need to prepare ourselves." Then, leaving the Sliding Center after Day one to get back on the shuttle bus, they stopped and looked at the standings posted near the finish line. They saw how they were up by 44/100 of a second, which is a little like being ahead by four touchdowns at halftime. They looked at each other. "Okay, forget what I said earlier," Mesler said. "I guess this *is* going to be like the World Championships."

The other two American sleds did not fare as well. If the U.S. men were going to break through and finally win the 4-man gold, it would have to be USA-1. Napier crashed during the second heat, experienced a severe back problem, and had to withdraw. Kohn's sled was about a full second back and had no chance.

That night was torture. What made the wait even more excruciating is that, even with the big lead, even with the best driver, even with a dream team of push athletes, even with a sled tailor made for the track, their effort could still go off the rails. "It was like Christmas," Mesler says. "Remember when you were a kid and you knew your parent got the transformer, or whatever present that you wanted because you saw it in their closet? And you're 99.9% sure it's for you. But you can never be completely sure because it might be for a cousin or something. That's what it was like. It felt like Christmas Day, and we were going to see if this wonderful thing that was going to happen was actually for us."

The next morning dawned gray and drizzly. Mesler was the first one from Team Holcomb down to breakfast. In the cafeteria sitting together were Briglia, Shimer, and a whole host of other coaches. They looked stricken, as if they had been up for hours dealing with some horrible news. Mesler went and got his food and then went to join them. Whatever conversation there was came to a standstill when he approached. Mesler sat down and nobody said a word. "Why are you guys so weird?" Mesler asked them crossly. "Go ahead and talk; do what you were doing." Everyone laughed but were still too nervous to relax.

Before the third heat, Holcomb, never that vocal and certainly not in the mood to be the center of attention at that point, quietly advertised his legendary cool demeanor as he went about his pre-race routine of visualizing his way down the track. Tomasevicz, on the other hand, had adrenaline to spare. "I'm pretty emotional; and since I didn't have to worry about driving like Holcomb or managing us push athletes like

Mesler, I was free to pipe up and get us psyched up before the race," he says. "I was pumped, to say the least."

The slower conditions for the third heat saw every team's time creep up, including Team Holcomb, which was .33 seconds slower than its second heat – but their lead increased by a hundredth of a second. The Night Train's .45 of a second cushion after three heats meant that the push athletes just had to load into the sled without falling, and Holcomb had to get them down without crashing, and the gold would be theirs. In the final run of a bobsled competition, the starting order goes from 20th place to 1st place. Team Holcomb would be the last sled down in the competition.

Between the third and fourth heats, Holcomb sat alone in his bubble, in his own world. He thought to himself: "No big deal. You've done this a thousand times before. Let's just do it again." Suddenly he was approached. It was none other than Lange, who patted him on the shoulder and sat down. He looked at Holcomb and didn't say anything for a few seconds. He smiled. "Don't worry man, you've got this," Lange told his rival. "Do it one more time."

This extraordinary moment might have been one of most generous gestures in Olympic history, or a seriously cynical move on Lange's part. But Holcomb chooses to believe that it was a great athlete who knew he had been beat acknowledging the long, arduous road that Holcomb and his push athletes had traveled to reach Lange's level of excellence. "Maybe he came up to me because I was looking nervous, I don't know," Holcomb says laughing. "But having one of the most decorated bobsledders ever, and someone you're about to beat, come over you and try to comfort you, it's a pretty big moment."

In the final run, the Night Train was the last sled down the track. It was clear after the start sequence — a good solid push, no mishaps — that nothing short of a Holcomb blackout going into the 50/50 turn would prevent the Night Train team from winning the gold medal. For Olsen, he just didn't want to do anything stupid like stick his head up or let go of the sled. "When we got through 50/50, that's when I knew we had won gold," Olsen says. "I was just trying not to take my hands off the handles." In the NBC broadcast booth, Morgan and his broadcast partner, Bob Papa, were committed to letting the pictures tell the story. "The only question in your mind when you're calling that race is if the moment is going too big for them," Papa recalls. They had the sled; they had the experience, the only question was whether they would be able to lay it all on the line that day." Both knew that once the Night Train was through the 50/50 turn – which Holcomb had named, of course – the race would be over. As they approached the turn, Morgan told the viewers that there was, "Only one more albatross on this track that could prevent Holcomb from the gold medal, and that's the 50-50 turn." After Morgan called out, "Through," it was over. He didn't have to say another word.

As Mesler peaked up after they crossed the finish line, the clock read 51.32 seconds, more than fast enough for a comfortable win. Next to the time read-out, Mesler saw the big red, digital "1" next to the Night Train, indicating their 1st place finish. "It's at that point that you realize you've done this thing you've been working toward, and waiting for, your entire life," Mesler says.

Crossing the finish line, Holcomb didn't have the reaction he thought he would. He still held fast to the mentality that it was just another race. It was exciting to win – but it was exciting to win any race. Obviously, the sports psychologist had done a thorough job. "I wasn't emotional as I should have been," he says. 'But who knows? Had I not prepared that way, we might not have won. I mean, to this day, it hasn't sunk in that I'm an Olympic gold medalist."

In the NBC broadcasting booth, Morgan stopped talking after Holcomb negotiated the 50/50 turn, knowing that gold was certain. In fact, he had made a deal with his broadcasting partner, Bob Papa, that when the Americans got through 50/50, he let Papa bring the sled into the historic gold medal and let the scenes on the television speak for themselves. The Night Train celebrated at the finish with the flower ceremony, and there was Bodine, Cuneo, Shimer, Briglia, and Kurtz, along with many others who had been there for different phases of the Bo-Dyn Project. Mesler hopped over a railing and ran up to the bleachers. He found his parents, other family members, and friends. Kurze was also on the other side of the fence looking on as Team USA won its first men's Olympic bobsled gold medal in 62 years.

As Cuneo was savoring the win, a young man came up to him and congratulated him in broken English. It was the classy Lange, who had come to congratulate Cuneo and the entire Bo-Dyn effort. "That was just totally cool," Cuneo said. "He's a great champion and a great guy."

The final results were posted. The Night Train, as USA-1, won Olympic Gold. Lange, with his German-1 sled registering a significantly faster run in the final heat than the Night Train, took silver. The hometown Canadian 4-man sled piloted by Lyndon Rush, with far more runs on the Vancouver track than any other team, took the bronze, finishing behind Lange by .01 hundredths of a second.

For Holcomb, his main sensation was a relief. Since he'd watched Tommy Moe win the gold medal in the men's downhill in Lillehammer in 1994, he'd wanted that gold medal. Holcomb was carrying that stress with him, and it was probably heavier because of the expectations surrounding the Night Train. Between his eye disease, the comeback, and the current success, there was a lot of closure to come to grips with. "You don't realize the weight you are carrying, and the toll it is taking until it's gone," Holcomb says. "There was a moment after we won, a few minutes later, when I said, "I did it. I'm a gold medalist. I never have to do that again.'"

Holcomb, Mesler, Tomasevicz and Olsen had won the last American gold medal of the Vancouver Games. That Tuesday, the latest *Sports Illustrated* cover came out with the boys on the cover. They did Letterman. The Today show called, and they did that show as well, after a night of celebrating at USA House. Bobsledding, for a few days, was front and center in the American sporting psyche with the first 4-man gold since 1948. Even the team that had last achieved this feat in St. Moritz—Francis Tyler, Patrick Martin,

Edward Rimkus, and William D'Amico—were cited in various media. "It was crazy," Holcomb says. "Today I can walk anywhere in the U.S., and no one recognizes me; but for a while after the gold, we were everywhere as a team and people would recognize us, stop us on the street, buy us drinks. I wouldn't want that all the time, but it was fun!"

For Geoff Bodine, who was on the deck at the Whistler Sliding Center for the final heat, being there for Olympic gold vindicated nearly 20 years of devotion to the cause. "To me, it was never the case that we wouldn't have been successful if we hadn't gotten the gold," Bodine says. "But that sure was sweet. You know, I have had my successes. But to see these Americans athletes do it as a team at the Olympics in our sleds, well — words can't describe it."

The 48 hours after the victory was a time of pure celebration. The best thing about it for Bodine is that different people who had been involved in the Bo-Dyn Project for a decade or even far longer were present. Brent Feldman, Holcomb's agent, saw how much Bodine enjoyed it all. "For Geoff, it was pure elation," Feldman says. "Seeing him with everyone, shedding a few tears, it was the culmination of a lot of work by a lot of people."

Bodine experienced a feeling he hadn't had in a little while – fun. For some reason, Bodine was struck with the memory of the gymkhanas he used to drive in, those parking lots races he'd compete in as a college student, racing around cones just driving regular street cars. For a long time when visitors would come to Bodine's home, they'd ask what these little awards were next to his Daytona Trophy. All those years later, Bodine kept his gymkhana trophies in an honored spot. There was nothing professional about it; it was just fun. And watching those guys go down in the Night Train reminded him again what fun was.

After the racing had ended, some competitors from other countries recognized Bodine and thanked him. That was a huge show of respect, because in racing — whether it's bobsledding or NASCAR — no one wants to get beat. By improving what a bobsled could be, by making them safe and faster and better looking, their national federations had to keep up, as well. Geoff Bodine had contributed more to the sport than he ever knew.

As for the Bo-Dyn Board – Bodine, Cuneo, Kurze, Goodwin, Morgan, and Vester – their job was complete. After the Night Train had taken the gold, they watched the four athletes receiving their gold medal in downtown Whistler in front of 6,000 people. Morgan watched alone in the huge crowd, having run over late from his NBC broadcasting duties; but after the ceremony had ended, they all gathered outside together in front of the hotel, taking in the cold Canadian air, the next challenge in life waiting.

Bo-Dyn Bobsled Project Mission Statement

- *To sponsor and promote design, technology, engineering, and manufacturing of products made in the USA through the construction of bobsleds to be used in international competition.*

- *To provide a forum of public education through the leverage of sponsorship and promotion to increase awareness of bobsledding both nationally and internationally.*